"A practical and down-to-earth guide to organizational change for not only seasoned leaders but also young professionals beginning their leadership journeys."

— **MARTY EVANS,** retired Rear Admiral, United States Navy; former National Executive Director, Girl Scouts of the USA; and former President and CEO, American Red Cross

"*Turnaround* is a must-read for anyone hoping to transform an organization."

— **TIM SMUCKER,** Chairman Emeritus, The J.M. Smucker Co.

"If your organization or project needs a new direction, Lisa Gable offers a wealth of practical advice for how to change course. An eye-opening guide to a spectacularly hard topic."

— **PAULA SANTILLI,** CEO, PepsiCo Latin America

"When I need help solving a tough problem, Lisa Gable is always one of my first calls."

— **AUREN HOFFMAN,** CEO of SafeGraph

"A wise, engaging book on how to solve big, seemingly intractable problems."

— **DAVID BUNNING,** former Chairman, FARE Board of Directors and private investor

"*Turnaround* reveals how working with others is one of the most effective ways to course-correct an organization that has lost its way."

— **TOSHIAKI (TAG) TAGUCHI,** former President and CEO, Toyota Motor North America, Inc.

"Lisa Gable's methodic and compassionate approach will help you transform even the most troubled of situations. A must-read."

— **KIM NELSON,** Independent Board Director, Colgate-Palmolive

"An incredibly practical and insightful book."

— **HEIDI ROIZEN,** Silicon Valley executive, venture capitalist, and entrepreneur

"If you are in a leadership role in any kind of business or organization, you should read this book."

— **RICHARD "RIC" JURGENS,** Chairman Emeritus, Hy-Vee, Inc.

"Lisa Gable's ability to solve difficult problems and transform any organization makes *Turnaround* a must-read."

— **ROB REID,** author and entrepreneur

"Lisa Gable's proven guidance for turning around teams and organizations by applying a unique combination of discipline with diplomacy and humanity is unquestionable. This book is both timely and essential for any business or team wishing to successfully navigate the challenging times ahead."

— **DOV BARON,** Inc Magazine Top 100 Leadership Speaker, Inc #1 Podcast for Fortune 500 Executives

"Expertly written, well-organized, and accessible, *Turnaround* is an illuminating read for anyone tasked with improving a project or partnership."

— **THOMAS SILVERA,** CST, Co-Founder and President of the Elijah-Alavi Foundation Inc.

"Lisa builds on a career straddling corporate, nonprofit, and government sectors to make a positive difference in the lives of millions. That passion for impact shines through in her book."

— **DR. DEREK YACH,** President of the Foundation for a Smokefree World, and former Cabinet Member of the World Health Organization

"If you need to solve a complex problem, Lisa Gable's book is a must-read. It provides a powerful framework for establishing trust, bringing partners to the table, and turning around any troubled venture."

— **DR. JERRY GIAQUINTA,** Academic Director for the World Bachelor in Business Program and Professor at USC Marshall School of Business

"Few people are better positioned to show us how to grapple with disruptive challenges and turn them into positive results than Lisa Gable. In *Turnaround*, she shares what she does brilliantly and intuitively and, in the process, gives us the gift of an insider's leadership guide."

— **SYLVIA ACEVEDO,** Corporate Director and former CEO, Girl Scouts of the USA

"There is a great reason that Lisa has been tapped, repeatedly, for presidential appointments, ambassadorships, and executive placements over the last thirty years; she is well known by business and policy leaders as a leader who can execute in challenging circumstances. Lisa Gable's *Turnaround* is an important read for inspiring and aspiring leaders as they guide their organizations and team members through the complexities of the ever-changing business and cultural climate."

— **CORDELL CARTER,** Executive Director, Socrates Program, The Aspen Institute

"Lisa's bipartisanship, leadership, and relationships across multiple sectors put her in the perfect position to help those seeking to improve their performance or outcomes."

— **MARY KATE CARY,** Presidential Speechwriter and Adjunct Professor, University of Virginia

TURNAROUND

TURNAROUND

HOW TO CHANGE COURSE WHEN THINGS ARE GOING SOUTH

LISA GABLE

IDEAPRESS
PUBLISHING

IDEAPRESS
PUBLISHING

Published in the United States by Ideapress Publishing.
Ideapress Publishing | www.ideapresspublishing.com

Cover Design by Molly Von Borstel, Faceout Studio
Interior Design by Paul Nielsen, Faceout Studio

ISBN: 978-164687-058-5

Special Sales
Ideapress Books are available at a special discount for bulk
purchases for sales promotions and premiums, or for use
in corporate training programs. Special editions, including
personalized covers, a custom foreword, corporate imprints,
and bonus content, are also available.

To my husband,
who makes me laugh,
and my daughter,
who makes me proud.

CONTENTS

TURNAROUND

INTRODUCTION

The Turnaround Method

You are sitting in a conference room at eight o'clock at night, and you can't see the light at the end of the tunnel. The engineers in your team are reworking the timeline, and once again, the product will not be shipping on time. You keep running the numbers, but they don't add up. Your boss is going to be upset.

The campaign team huddles at a Starbucks away from headquarters. The new press secretary—the last one left a week ago—is agitated as she finds out the donor event that evening won't be full. The gubernatorial race started strong, but now things seem to be going nowhere. The incumbent keeps losing ground and going off message. Get-out-the-vote efforts are disorganized. Grassroots volunteers, frustrated that their time is used poorly, stop showing up. A loss seems inevitable.

The board of a nonprofit wraps up a long day. The CEO has kept the organization afloat, but it's lost momentum. The nonprofit spends more money than it brings in through donors. It is not having the impact it used to, and its community is not as engaged. Is it even worth resuscitating?

Every day, projects, teams, and organizations find themselves stuck with a seemingly intractable problem. The product is on life support and bleeding money. The team is exhausted by never-ending drama. The organization is hobbled by competition. A revolving door of project leads, managers, consultants, and leaders tried to fix the problem. No one seems to be able to turn the situation around.

During the past thirty-five years, I have seen scenarios like these play out time and time again. I have seen the frustration and stress that good teams suffer when they feel they are spinning their wheels for nothing. I have seen leaders execute one strategy after another in a panic, trying to salvage organizations and programs they've poured their hearts and souls into. When things go south, course-correcting is not always easy. You can have all the resources at your disposal—a big budget, lots of people—and still fail to right a ship going in the wrong direction.

I know this because people call me when they don't know where else to turn. I have been asked to turn around businesses whose customers are leaving for the competition, operational units that aren't reaching their goals, political campaigns that are heading down the path to "too close to call," and nonprofits whose faltering impact is losing donors. I've also been brought in to start things from scratch and solve problems that others have not cracked. From Silicon Valley to Washington, D.C., I have seen it all.

For the past three decades, I've been honing my approach for turning around failing projects, teams, and organizations, as well as for solving seemingly intractable problems. My method, which I share in the chapters that follow, has been deeply influenced by lessons I was fortunate to learn early in my career—in my job at process-obsessed Intel and from my father, who built a university from the ground up with grace and heart. Straightforward but rigorous, the method marries discipline with diplomacy. Best of all, it can be deployed in virtually any situation where a turnaround is needed.

WHY THINGS GO SOUTH

I've always loved fixing things. I like managing complexity and coming up with solutions to messy problems. It's a skill I learned from one of my first mentors, Craig Barrett, former CEO of Intel. When I started working as Craig's technical assistant at age twenty-five, he was senior vice president of manufacturing at the growing semiconductor company. Craig showed me how to apply engineering processes to solve problems in any setting. He helped me understand the importance of having quality improvement processes, of benchmarking against best-of-class competitors, and of managing complexity by using data. He taught me how to break down complex problems and how to use systems to build sustainable futures.

Needless to say, Craig had an indelible impact on my management style and on my approach to problem-solving. In fact, every turnaround experience I will share with you in this book was operationally based on manufacturing techniques I learned working at Intel under Craig. Most important, Craig taught me that to solve a complex problem, you must turn it on its head. You should ignore the popular recommendations or knee-jerk reactions for how to solve it. Instead, you must try relentlessly to understand the *underlying cause of the problem*—especially if no one has been able to fix it after many attempts. He taught me, for example, to call our hotline over and over to understand why customers might be having less than great experiences. Once his earlier advice led me to physically search through Intel's mailrooms in Europe to understand how the process for mailing hard copies of documents from the United States to our international offices might have been affecting communications.

In my work as a turnaround specialist, I've had the chance to look under the hood of countless organizations and projects as I tried to understand the underlying cause of their problems. Here are the seven most common reasons why projects, teams, and organizations go south:

They Are Built on Haphazardly Designed Processes and Structures. Things can go south when an organization, team, or project grows too quickly with little planning. For example, say a company rushes to scale too soon following a merger or acquisition, or a project's scope keeps getting bigger as new managers take over. When a team finds early success, its budget is expanded, allowing it to add more people in a hurry. As these entities expand, they start looking like houses that have been added onto without rhyme or reason: a porch here, an extra wing there, chimneys where no one could have imagined them.

As new owners move in, they continue tweaking a less than well-planned organizational architecture. A merger may have allowed a company to grow rapidly, but now the organization's systems are poorly integrated or its overlapping product lines are leading to customer confusion. New managers may believe that increasing the scope of the project gives them more influence and power in the organization. However, they fail to consider the inefficiencies they've built into the project every time it gets bigger. A major donor's gift allows a nonprofit team to hire more people. With a larger head count, they can expand services to new groups or demographics. But the nonprofit's impact diffuses as it tries to be too many things to too many people.

Those in Charge Believe More Money Can Solve Everything. As the nonprofit example shows, sometimes the fundamentally wrong assumption that underpins stalled projects, teams, or organizations is that money can fix anything. When a company experiences a challenge, it's not uncommon for its leader to throw money at it as a solution. However, the company often fails to add enough process controls to drive lasting, systematic changes. So the fix fails, the problem grows, and the leader keeps throwing money at it, on and on.

I learned early in my career that when a greater sum of money is immediately available, people take less care with it and tend to make larger messes. Throwing money at the problem is typically nothing more than a quick fix—one that often comes with an "It's not that hard" attitude. It makes it all too easy for teams to avoid solving problems creatively. In contrast, lean organizations quickly learn to find unique and collaborative solutions that lead to more powerful and sustainable results.

The Economics of the Business Make the End Goal Impossible. Many organizations are led by people who lack the political aptitude to anticipate how regulations can inhibit their ability to innovate at a competitive pace. They fail to monitor quasi-governmental bodies such as the World Trade

Organization or the World Health Organization and to recognize early how the policy stances these bodies advocate might hamper the organizations' ability to grow. The result? They are caught flat-footed. They try to fight the regulations, or they retreat when they should engage with their critics and collaboratively come up with creative solutions that work for everyone.

They Are Stuck in a Cookie-Cutter Approach to Culture and Management. Sometimes intractable problems appear when those in charge identify and pursue a prototype of experience—an organizational culture, management style, or leadership approach—that has worked in the past but may not be compatible with new realities. For example, some organizations continue to hire and promote mainly men—members of the "good old boy club"—to their top ranks. Today we recognize that to solve problems creatively, you need as many diverse voices working on them as possible. As many organizations struggle with diversity, equity, inclusion, and access, their inability to innovate competitively becomes more pronounced.

Their Leaders Make Self-Interested and Empire-Building Decisions. Hubris is part of human nature and the root of many problems, dating back to the Roman Empire and Old Testament stories. Some managers and leaders prioritize their career goals and focus on strategic moves that benefit them personally—making them look better or giving them more power—rather than on decisions that lead to a healthy and sustainable project, team, or organization.

Their Founders Overstay Their Welcome. Many projects and organizations suffer management challenges as they grow, and these challenges can persist when the founders stick around a bit too long. Charismatic founders are often great visionaries, but they don't always have the ability to execute. Their disproportionate level of influence may reduce an organization's effectiveness and perpetuate problems. Sometimes their *enfant terrible* or "eccentric genius" behaviors can wreck good business ideas.

Founder's Syndrome isn't just a start-up issue. It's frequently found in the nonprofit world and in churches where founders who view process as a nuisance sometimes elevate their own vision above everything else. They recruit weak boards to ensure that there is little oversight—only to land themselves and their institutions in scandals. Because their boards or investors can be overly personally invested in the organization's success, they often let the bad behavior slide.

Their Leaders Don't Recognize the Project, Team, or Organization Is at an End Point.

Sometimes a project or organization outlives its usefulness. Yet some executives and boards continue to prop up the project or organization when they should accept it's over, celebrate its accomplishments, and either shut the doors or merge with a stronger entity.

This is particularly common in nonprofits, where a belief in the organization's "higher purpose" overshadows the reality that *all* organizations are driven by market forces: Regardless of whether you are a for-profit or nonprofit, you need to take in more money than you spend. Families who start nonprofits or CEOs who sit on the boards of nonprofits they care deeply about often lack experience in the philanthropy world and hesitate to apply sound business principles when managing them. Their decisions—or their willingness to overlook poor decisions by those managing the nonprofit—are driven by emotion, not by the practicalities of the market.

I experienced this while serving on the board of a business graduate school. Although the school was recognized as one of the top five programs in its category, it was in severe financial distress. After a few board meetings, it became apparent to me that fellow board members who were alumni could not make objective decisions because of their love for the school. I recognized that we had no financial game plan, so I pushed hard for the school to explore a merger with another nationally recognized institution that shared a similar mission in international business. After I made the decision to leave the board, the school went through a failed buyout with a for-profit entity. Ultimately a soft landing was arranged through a major donor intervention, and the school was folded into another institution that was in the position to maximize its core curriculum and retain the program's positive reputation.

In 2020 and 2021, the COVID-19 pandemic caused massive disruption, exposing organizations and projects that were suffering from these seven problems and leaving them in even more perilous shape. When your project, team, or organization is built on haphazardly planned systems and processes, when you are stuck operating in outdated ways, and when your leaders make decisions from a place of ego and not with the entities' best interests at heart, a disruption of this kind can be the nail in the coffin. Sadly, for many, the pandemic was just that.

But it doesn't have to be this way. If your project, team, or organization is worth saving, you can turn it around, even in the direst situations.

DISCIPLINE AND DIPLOMACY

The method I've developed to turn around even the most troubled organizations is influenced in many ways by process engineering, a concept that I learned working with my mentor Craig Barrett in manufacturing in the early 1990s.

Back then, Silicon Valley was rising to global prominence, and process engineering was all the rage. Our bibles were Peter Senge's *The Fifth Discipline* and Andy Grove's *High Output Management*. Process engineering is all about understanding and designing your business processes and work flows so they operate at their best. The goal is to optimize the workings of your organization by improving output while cutting costs.

As technology moved away from building physical products to building software, process engineering went out of favor and gave way to improvisation and agile development. When you are building software or websites that can be changed seemingly in an afternoon, process is seen as bureaucratic.

However, when things start to blow up, discipline is critical to digging your way out. You need to examine your process carefully and understand both what is working and can stay, and what is not and needs to go. My turnaround method not only brings back this discipline of process engineering, but also adds another important element that I learned from my father: diplomacy.

Like Craig, my father was a builder, even-tempered and direct. He built an institution from 150 people to a nationally recognized university that today staffs around 7,500 people. He believed that every crisis allowed the institution to define an even stronger trajectory for the future. He intentionally and purposefully designed the fundamentals of the business in a manner that was sustainable, supported large-scale growth, and contributed to the long-term economic health of the region.

But above all, he took great care to develop relationships. For my father, growth was a team sport. He believed in building an army of supporters instead of imposing his will through financial or political strength. He built bridges across religions, countries, and political parties. His openness to a cross section of opinions made people of all backgrounds and philosophical stripes comfortable working with him.

A self-made and self-directed man, my father was humble. Since he experienced life's challenges at an early age, he always sought out those who weren't natural stars or didn't come from wealth or exceptional means. With his extra support and encouragement, they would become the leaders they were meant to be. Within the organization he led, my father carefully but compassionately moved people through stages of their career—even if it meant an individual wasn't going to advance to the next level. Combining kindness and grace, he listened to people and then worked with them to outline the major milestones that would help them achieve their objectives. He was thoughtful and always respectful.

After he died, we heard from hundreds of people whose lives he had touched—students, teachers, coaches, CEOs, news anchors, pro athletes, philanthropists, elected officials, parents, ministers, and business leaders. His attention and dedication to helping others achieve their dreams were apparent in their stories and remembrances.

My father is my role model for a results-driven yet diplomatic management philosophy. By blending his graceful, big-hearted leadership style with Intel's methodical, process-driven approach, I've been able to turn around complex projects, teams, and organizations of all sizes in almost every industry and sector. You can, too, with the turnaround method.

THE TURNAROUND METHOD

In the next few chapters, I will take you through the four straightforward but rigorous steps that you must take to pull off a successful turnaround:

Step 1. Visualize the future. Stop thinking of the problem and tweaking what's already there. Instead, focus on where you want to end—on your future perfect scenario.

Step 2. Break down the past. Analyze what is working today and can help bring your new future to life—and what is not and needs to go.

Step 3. Create a path from present to future. Map out the critical decisions that you need to make—and build the right team to move forward with them.

Step 4. Execute with speed, confidence, and heart. Set aggressive goals and partner well so you can speed ahead to your goal. You've got a plan—now run with it.

Although this method may appear simple, it demands strength and conviction. It's not easy to point your compass in a new direction and change course. It requires making bold decisions, adhering to a process that many around you will resist, and being open to collaborating with others. If you commit to the method, it can work for you as it has for me.

My turnaround method has been thoroughly battle-tested. It's proven applicable and relevant over the years as I've used it to help organizations surmount challenges that major economic inflection points such as the dot-com boom, the dot-com bust, the Great Recession, and the global pandemic have thrown their way. I have used it to lead turnarounds in government organizations, businesses, and global public-private partnerships and nonprofits. This method can even help you turn around intractable problems or issues that have baffled others.

My first turnaround, in fact, was not of a failed organization or project, but rather in finding a way to change the course of an issue that seemed to have no straightforward solution.

After Craig was promoted to COO of Intel, the first project he assigned to me was evaluating and improving Intel's impact on K-12 education. Craig felt passionate about education. He understood that Intel's success—and that of the U.S. tech industry—depended on its talent. However, the pool for qualified, talented engineers was not nearly as big as it needed to be (and still isn't). Craig thought that Intel ought to address the deepest source of the talent pool problem: K-12 education. Without stronger STEM education in science, technology, engineering, and mathematics, not enough students would have the mathematics background to pursue STEM degrees and become engineers.

Back then, companies didn't have corporate social responsibility programs; philanthropy in Silicon Valley was fairly unsophisticated. At Intel, site managers had control over how they supported local charities and community projects. They often donated money to local schools, and their employees who cared deeply about education took time off work to teach or help design STEM programs for schoolchildren. Yet Intel had no idea whether these decentralized efforts were moving the needle in the right direction or how much they were costing.

The future we visualized was one in which Intel took a seat at the education reform table by creating a model for how tech companies could advance K-12 STEM education. Convincing all those site managers to join us in this journey—essentially using shuttle diplomacy to talk them out of money they were using to fund their local pet projects—was not an easy task for a young woman in a mostly male environment in the 1990s.

I started by looking under the hood of how site managers were handling their community philanthropy in education. I examined every process, every program, and every contribution to understand and identify the ad hoc engagements that were having an impact and that I could use somehow to make our future a reality—and those that were not. For years, Intel volunteers had informally advised teachers and local schools on STEM education as a unique asset. I realized that sharing our process management expertise with educators and school administrators through a formal public-private partnership would be the key to achieving our goals.

Eventually Intel executed on this strategy by co-creating and co-managing a public elementary school, Kyrene de la Mirada Elementary School in Chandler, Arizona. It would serve as a prototype for how the tech industry could support and influence STEM education. We applied fundamental Intel manufacturing principles such as site-based management when designing the school. Intel senior managers participated in a special committee, which included the superintendent and other leaders in the school district, to track the school's progress and move any boulders out of the way. Intel also provided training on effective meeting techniques and team management processes, and later it provided training and work opportunities to help teachers learn continuous-improvement management processes. Along our journey, we partnered with other private organizations such as financial consultant Arthur Andersen and think tank Rand Corporation to tap their expertise.

Using Kyrene de la Mirada as a model, we were able to scale into larger public-private partnerships that involved whole public school districts, Intel training groups, corporate partners, and even government institutions such as the National Laboratories. Together we were able to achieve exponential growth for our private partnership educational model, eventually receiving national attention and qualifying for a multi-million-dollar National Science Foundation grant.

We made our vision a reality: Intel made a measurable impact in K-12 STEM and held a seat at the education reform table. Twenty-five years later, I am proud to say that Kyrene de la Mirada continues to excel in STEM and leadership and is listed consistently as one of Arizona's top schools.

In the next few chapters, I will share stories of three other turnarounds, explain each step of the turnaround method, and show how you can deploy it to make positive and lasting change.

HOW TO LEAD A SUCCESSFUL TURNAROUND

If your project, team, or organization has gone off the rails or fallen into a position that is unsustainable long term, this book is for you. You may be the CEO of a for-profit or nonprofit organization, the head of a major division or program, the manager of a team, or the lead on a project tasked with heading its turnaround. Or you may be an individual contributor who sees an opportunity to make things better. Regardless of your title, this is your moment to assume the mantle of leadership and become a driver of positive change. Stop looking over your shoulder for someone else to save the day. You may be the hero.

As you begin leading a turnaround, consider these five recommendations:

- Start the turnaround process without assumptions. If you go into a turnaround with a predetermined outcome in mind, you might miss

what really is making your project or organization fail. Avoid falling for the assumption that
things are going south because the last person in charge didn't know what he or she was
doing. A leadership change won't miraculously
resolve everything. The underlying cause of
the problem is likely more complicated: The
fundamentals of the project or business might
be broken. Instead, remain open-minded about
what might turn around the problem. Listen
to people, internally and externally. Hear what
your team members have to say, internalize
their viewpoints, and incorporate all that you
have learned into a cohesive strategy. In particular, listen to your customers and partners.
What is important to them? What can you do
to make their life less difficult? How can you
give them a better return on their investment
or their time?

- Take the time to engage in shuttle diplomacy.
  The turnaround method I'll teach you requires
  a radical restructuring of your organization,
  team, or project. That can be overwhelming
  for team members, especially those who dread

change. They may shut down or build walls if they believe that you don't respect all the good that was done before you arrived. It's easy to get frustrated with people whom we perceive as being in the way of our vision. But rather than antagonize them, take the time to help them move forward with you rather than against you. Change does not happen overnight; you'll need people on your side to get this done!

- Find like-minded people to help achieve your vision. Sometimes you'll need to bring in people who are from outside your team or are not entrenched in the industry to help achieve your vision. Find people who not only are process-driven and energized by the turnaround method, but also have compassion and lack ego—traits that will inspire loyalty.

- Don't treat every step like a battle. Turnarounds are a process, not a war. You definitely want to become the best-in-class, but your actions should focus on improving your competitive capabilities through aggressive, sustainable goals, not by pummeling your competitors with back-channel maneuvers. Engaging in personal attacks or undercutting your opponents might work well in a Jeffrey Archer novel, but it can strew rubble in your path and allow more nimble competitors to step into the void and steal your market share.

- Keep your commitments. My father used to say, "Don't hand someone the gun to shoot you." He believed leaders have no margin for error: The smallest things can trip them up and make others question their reliability. My dad taught me that you show up when you say you are going to show up—no matter how tired you are. You do everything you said you would do—no matter how inconvenient it is.

Change is hard. Leading change is even harder. You'll have to be tough to get through likely bumps along the way. But the reward—leading a successful turnaround with grace and resolve—is worth it.

When my father died in 2019, I found a letter he had written to me. It has inspired me to share my experiences and hope they will inspire you when you are charging up the hill, fighting to make your vision a reality: *"Remember to look beyond what is currently in your life and try to visualize what is unseen. Count your blessings, and it will also help you challenge the crisis you are experiencing. Some of the greatest stumbling blocks I have ever faced have also resulted in being my greatest steppingstones."*

STEP 1

VISUALIZE THE FUTURE

Stop Thinking about the Problem and Focus on Where You Want to End

In 2008, Indra Nooyi, then CEO of PepsiCo, stood on stage at an industry event, frustrated by a brewing political battle that threatened her company and others in the food and beverage industry. One-third of Americans were overweight or obese.[1] Skyrocketing health care costs were being traced to medical issues exacerbated by weight: hypertension, diabetes, and heart disease, to name a few.

Nooyi knew that U.S. food and beverage makers had already changed their recipes, reducing sugars and fats across many products. However, there was no mechanism in place to track these changes, so no one knew what good work they were doing. As a result, skeptical government officials and key public health influencers blamed them for the looming health crisis. Hints of regulation, taxation, and litigation dominated conversation in Washington, D.C., and state capitals.

As she stood in front of her peers, Nooyi went off script. She demanded that other companies join her in coming up with a solution. She not only warned companies that they would face increasing backlash if they didn't, but also reminded them that they owned part of the responsibility to help solve the obesity crisis. Fifteen of her peers heard the call and joined PepsiCo in creating a committee to work on the problem.

These sixteen CEOs held long planning meetings, but for eighteen months, they struggled and argued. They poured millions into small-scale ideas that failed. They hired the famed McKinsey consulting firm, which came up with an idea too complex and expensive to scale. When they decided to hire someone to lead the effort, the CEOs brought in people from public health and industry, but all their conversations were about tweaking the existing solutions. If we just did this a little better, then maybe our political opponents would back off. If we put a lot of money into getting kids to exercise, then we would solve the problem.

Finally, they reached out to me. I did not come from public health. I knew nothing about the food and beverage industry. However, I came with an open mind and a blank slate. I simply asked these exhausted executives, "What is the most important problem you need to solve? What do you want your perfect future to look like?"

The answer was clear: The CEOs wanted a cease-fire with public health and regulators. The discord between the two had grown increasingly acrimonious since the late 1990s and needed to end. These two groups despised each other. Instead, they wanted to engage directly with the Robert Wood Johnson Foundation (RWJF), one of the most respected organizations and leaders in public health. Dr. Risa Lavizzo-Mourey, the foundation's CEO, had made it clear that consumer products companies could no longer ignore, tweak, or lobby their way out of their responsibility: After all, they made the food that people were eating.

As I talked with them over the next few weeks, it became obvious that they needed to commit to an "Apollo" project, a big, bold plan with measurable results. They needed to establish a well-defined goal, a time frame, and a commitment to fund their efforts. The time for tweaks was over.

That Apollo project would turn out to be the Healthy Weight Commitment Foundation (HWCF), a large-scale public-private partnership that I would lead. It was set up with a five-year timeline to realize these companies' perfect future and with an upfront budget of three years. HWCF would have the power and flexibility to negotiate with allies in the public health community without the engagement of the sixteen member companies—the ability to be independent from market motivations and to be 100 percent transparent was critical to its credibility. By focusing on a bold future, HWCF would fundamentally rethink how food and beverage companies could gain the trust of the public and the public health leaders that had eluded them for years.

As things are going south on a project or organization, we often get stuck, even obsessed, on specific issues or problems. We think that if we could only fix this or that, we would be able to turn this ship around. So we tweak what's already there to make it work better. When that doesn't work, we tweak another thing. The churn continues.

Although it is always good to pinpoint what's not working, focusing on fixing existing problems is not the best starting point for a successful turnaround. You can become so focused on resolving the issues in front of your nose or pointing fingers at each other that you never resolve the underlying issues affecting your results. If your project or organization has coded a few times on the operating table, something is either fundamentally wrong with its overall design or position in the marketplace, or the economics of your business no longer work.

Stop thinking about your present problems and start imagining where you want your project, organization, or team to end up in the future—then design a path to this new vision. To visualize the future, you must:

- Describe your perfect world scenario.
- Identify Job 1 (...and 2 and 3).
- Reframe success.
- Evangelize your future vision.

By taking these four steps, you will sidestep existing operational assumptions that are cluttering your mind.

You will break free from the distractions of the daily grind and any restrictive parameters in current operations. You will be able to reflect and redirect your abilities to designing around a future that maximizes your team's or organization's expertise and creativity.

Whether you are managing your first turnaround or your third, it is likely that your capabilities and expertise placed you in a position to effect change in a positive way. Someone either chose you to solve the problem, or you had some bad luck and are now stuck with it. No matter the reason you find yourself in the driver's seat, it's your moment to step up and show your leadership skills. Your first task: to picture a "perfect world scenario" for your project, organization, or team.

DESCRIBE YOUR PERFECT WORLD SCENARIO

When I meet someone who is struggling with a project or an organization, I ask him or her, "If you could wave your magic wand, what is the future you would want to see?" In other words, describe to me the perfect world scenario you want as your end point. This scenario can be as bold as you'd like.

Over the years, I've learned that this scenario typically leverages and maximizes a core competency that your project or organization is uniquely qualified in and that drives your position of strength. The first step to describe a future perfect world scenario is, paradoxically, to go back to the past. Understanding your project's or organization's genesis can be the key to rediscovering its core competency.

Your Core Competency

Your project, organization, or group came into existence for a reason. Whoever founded it came together around a particular purpose. Probably they did not believe that other organizations or competitors were providing an effective offering or solving a particular problem, so they started something new. Go back to the charter, the meeting minutes or emails, the original business plan, or the past board books of the project, organization, or group you are tasked with turning around to understand the purpose behind its creation. If that purpose or that big problem is still relevant today, then you are still in business.

That's precisely what Steve Jobs did in 1996 when he returned to rescue Apple. The company had lost its edge, unable to deliver breakthrough products since its Macintosh line of personal computers debuted in 1984. When Jobs came back, he knew there was a market for easy, accessible computer products. He immediately centered the business around Apple's "special sauce": exceptional design focused on simplicity. That focus resulted in industry-changing products, from the best-selling iMac (favored by first-time PC users) to the iPod, iTunes, and of course, the iPhone.

You too must find the special sauce or core competency that will enable you to reposition yourself as the market leader or become *the* internal project, team, or program that can solve a big need or problem. Evaluate your competitors. Outline what they do, what you do, and which has a higher probability of success. Then identify overlaps between you and them. You may have a particular technology, partnerships, or existing infrastructure that would be costly for others to replicate and be competitive. You may have an expertise or access to a treasure trove of data that makes your project unique. Zero in on what you can do that others cannot. This is your core competency—and the key to your perfect world scenario.

Your Perfect World Scenario

With your core competency in mind, you can visualize a fresh future for your organization, project, or program. This perfect world scenario might be one where you leverage your core competency to mitigate a rising risk that has a negative impact on your customer base, constituency, or community. Or it might be one in which your core competency allows you to solve a problem that threatens your position in the market. Or perhaps your core competency (say, a breakthrough technology) will transform the way people live or work.

To visualize a new future, it often helps to focus on your customers' or constituents' pain points. Often in an effort to build something great, we fail to appreciate what they truly want and need—and therefore what will lead to our success. It's like a software developer who keeps updating one of its products, now in decline, to "make it better." Sure, every update optimizes the product's performance or adds bells and whistles to it. But it also leads to error messages or prompts the end user to run endless updates that seem to pop up whenever he or she is right in the middle of an important task. The developer is so focused on improving the usability of its product that it fails to see the customer's perspective that the updates are getting in the way of getting work done.

What if instead this software developer visualizes a future in which a happy end user relies on its product to complete a task successfully, shut down the computer at five o'clock, and attend a child's soccer game? How could it turn around this failing product to allow this customer to do just that? It's probably not by sending constant software updates that interrupt the work. Perhaps the solution is not technical; perhaps the solution lies in providing customers who don't have the time or savvy to engage in complex computer updates the best-in-class software support.

All of us bring existing prejudices to how we approach problem-solving. Maybe the software developer can see only a technical solution to its failing product. Perhaps it cannot dig itself out of a hole because its organizational culture prioritizes technical issues and solutions, ignoring possible non-technical approaches or the viewpoints of non-technical staff. It is important that you continually test your assumptions and consider others' perspectives.

No other perspective is as important as your customers'. It's critical that you put yourself in the shoes of those your project, program, or organization is trying to serve and understand their experiences. Your new vision *has* to have a benefit for everyone involved. That's why whenever I'm engaged in solving a complex turnaround or problem, I try to "watch" in my head a movie reel of my customers' or end users' journey. Doing so makes the problem tangible, not theoretical. When we spend time visualizing the complexity of life for a person who is experiencing the actual problem we are meant to solve, we can begin to see what's missing and which gaps we can fill with our new vision.

Once you've visualized this new perfect world scenario, describe what it would look like in three years or five years or whatever time frame the scope of your turnaround demands and allows. Analyze the level of investment that will be needed to get there. Clearly identify all who would be affected by this new scenario. Perhaps your vision might negatively affect a customer segment or community you serve. Can you afford to lose them? Or do you need their support to achieve the future you envision?

Answering these questions will help you clarify the vision around which you will build your strategic plan. Don't get hung up on the details, though. At this point, simply lay out a high-level vision of the big plays required to achieve your perfect future state: Is it achievable with the current business model or design of your organization or project? Or will it require a major redesign?

When I started the Healthy Weight Commitment Foundation (HWCF) in 2009, at a basic level, the food and beverage companies, public health community, and government were in agreement about the fundamental issue: Americans were overweight. But to move forward, I had to get everyone—CEOs and public health experts—to agree to a joint vision. I never anticipated how rough those first twelve months would be and how hard wrangling agreements out of sixteen fierce market competitors would prove. Getting them and public health leaders to agree on a perfect world scenario was one of the toughest challenges of my career.

The assumption of many in public health was that the food industry benefited financially from selling higher-calorie products. Public health advocates argued that the industry was overselling some "healthier-for-you" alternatives as being healthier than they actually were, leading consumers to eat more of them. They also argued that food manufacturers were using cartoons to entice kids into asking their parents to buy higher-calorie products anyway.

Others in public health wondered if we, as a society, were just getting too lazy, depending on our cars to carry us a few blocks when we could easily walk. Still others thought that structural designs needed to change, for example, displaying less candy at the checkout counter or installing more bike lanes in major cities.

Perhaps it was all of these issues combined.

Our team at HWCF kept asking: What was the one thing we—the sixteen food and beverage manufacturers we represented—could do that no one else could do? The answer was unavoidable: We owned the "intake." We made a third of the food sold in the United States. That was the piece of the problem which we needed to solve. That was our core competency.

So we tried to visualize a new consumer life journey from the marketplace through the annual physical. We asked ourselves a series of questions: How could we affect people's eating habits through the journey? How should we make those changes while meeting the customers' needs for taste, value, and convenience? How would we ensure that underserved communities had access to healthier products?

The sixteen manufacturers sold a variety of products that ranged from beverages and snacks to pasta, ice cream, and frozen foods. We had to find a common metric across all of them that would allow us to answer the questions above: Should we reduce a specific nutrient from our products? Promote a specific diet with them? Everyone was hyper aware of the SnackWell effect—a product supposedly made healthier, in this case by reducing fat, that actually led to increased calorie consumption.

With the help of scientists from the Robert Wood Johnson Foundation, the nation's largest public health philanthropic organization, and from Campbell Soup Company, we landed on calories *sold*. Reducing the overall calories our companies sold—accomplished by producing and marketing new or reformulated lower-calorie products, as well as selling smaller packages—reduced the consumption of nutrients that cause weight gain and provided healthier food for *all* families.

Understanding the foundation's core competency— our ability to influence calories sold—allowed us to describe a perfect world scenario: Through a reduction in calories in the marketplace, the consumer's journey would be a path to a healthier life. Public health officials and the White House agreed that would be a good start in creating a market dynamic for positive change.

IDENTIFY JOB 1 (...AND 2 AND 3)

Your journey to delivering your perfect world scenario is possible only if you focus everyone on your team or project on a clearly articulated and easily understood objective.

As I learned early in my career, you can't do it all. In a turnaround, you have a limited number of plays in which you can invest time and resources heavily to execute your scenario. Job 1 is your big play, the boldest objective. For the Reagan administration, Job 1 was winning the Cold War. For Intel in the early 1990s, Job 1 focused on getting the tech industry to standardize around its platform. For Salesforce software, Job 1 was to change the way organizations managed and tracked relationships by building a company "around one main idea: that software should be delivered 24/7 to people over the cloud."[2]

In the case of HWCF, our perfect world scenario was reducing the number of calories sold to make healthier and lower-calorie foods more accessible and affordable to everyone. To make that happen, we had to set an audacious Job 1 that not only would make a difference but also would signal to the public health community our unquestionable commitment to becoming partners in finding solutions to the obesity epidemic. The members of HWCF pledged to reduce 1.5 *trillion* calories from products during the next five years. That was the change that would enable us to realize our future.

If Job 1 is the big-ticket item, you also will need to define Jobs 2 and 3, the key deliverables that will create the change. Think of them as the backup singers to your vocalist. For example, say you are an association for companies in a particular industry. Year after year, membership is falling. You know that companies can afford to join only a handful of associations, so they choose those they think will best support their ability to do business. Your core competency is the richness and expansiveness of your membership base—that's what sets you apart from other associations.

So you define Job 1 as expanding your organization's ability to drive business opportunities within different localities through a federated model. But to be effective, the organization can't just focus on Job 1. It also must meet some base requirements expected of any industry association: leading mandates in public affairs and advocacy (Job 2); and offering membership benefits, such as providing industry information or services like job boards (Job 3). How you create a strategic benefit within these baseline requirements will elevate your value to the members and ladder up to support your Job 1.

To define Jobs 1, 2, and 3, throw out really big ideas, pressure-test them, and identify where you are uniquely positioned to perform. Realizing your future can take a few years, but by establishing these overarching goals, you are moving forward in a systematic, measurable fashion. You want to think big but broad enough to allow continuous improvement.

You also want to ensure you are defining Jobs 1, 2, and 3 that are actionable, cost effective, and sustainable. Some Job 1's are amazing—but only if you can pull them off! You do not want to create an expense-to-revenue ratio that is unsustainable or define a Job 1 that depends on activities too expensive to replicate quarter after quarter or year after year. If you jump too fast and take on too much, you dilute your initial actions. So step back and recognize your boundaries and barriers. After all, you want to base your plans in the reality of the environment in which you operate.

Sometimes your perfect world scenario cannot be realized in the near future. For example, you might need to wait until a technology catches up, or a certain regulation passes, or a program or obligation can be properly phased out or met before it's canceled. As you create a road map to your future vision, you may have to blow up a few things before you can begin rebuilding. If this is the case, you may be looking at a staged approach—where you must recognize and remove barriers before you truly begin defining and executing against your primary goals (Jobs 1, 2, and 3).

Make sure to identify operational issues that stand in your way and establish milestones by which you plan to remove these barriers. Your team should have a clear picture of what pieces need to be actualized before your big idea can be realized. In the meantime, simplify and focus your limited assets on Job 1. Stay laser-focused on that goal, even if you have to zigzag around obstacles to achieve it.

The milestones you set for Job 1 will depend on the scope of your turnaround. Certain types of change have more predictable estimated timelines. You may have only six months to turn around a failing project, for example. But if you are turning around a whole organization and shifting its culture, you may need three to five years. Personally, I like to set tight timelines. I may set a major milestone at eighteen months, which is my rule of thumb for when a turnaround begins to emerge and show success.

My next milestones may be three years after, where I can stretch comfortably into our goals, and my end point might be at five years. This probably comes from my experience as a political appointee: You get only the time between four-year election cycles to achieve your objectives. If I am boxed in, I don't waste time. At HWCF, food and beverage member companies defined Job 1 as the reduction of 1.5 trillion calories in the marketplace. We established a timeline of five years to get it done.

Be aware that the time periods set for executing turnarounds—and therefore the Jobs 1, 2, and 3 that will get you there—are decreasing every day. Big companies are entering shorter cycles of innovation, and the market moves at dizzying speed. If you are helping create change within a corporate or organizational structure, you may be asked to up-level operations quickly.

Whether you have six months or five years to turn around your project, organization, or team, the key is to be realistic. Identify a logical end date for when you must show some successes and stick to it. Have a path to positivity that others have agreed to join you in. With a perfect world scenario in place, clearly defining Jobs 1, 2, and 3 will enable you to start crafting a high-level document that outlines your key objectives, the barriers that must be removed to accomplish them, and the financial investment and time required to reach your perfect world scenario.

REFRAME SUCCESS

If you are in the middle of a turnaround, that means the old standards of operating, measuring, and defining success are no longer working. It is time to hit the reset button. To do that, you need to define new basic operating standards for your organization, project, or program.

I have always worked for manufacturers—high tech, auto, and food and beverage. In each turnaround that I conducted, the basic operating standard I established is that we must increase deliverables while reducing costs. That is table stakes in a turnaround, no matter your industry or sector. If you are a tech company, you need to increase the value of your tech offerings while reducing costs. If you are a nonprofit, you need to increase the impact of your services or the influence of your advocacy while reducing costs. If you are running a project within your organization, you need to increase its effectiveness while reducing costs or resources, such as time invested.

When you are in the middle of a turnaround, it is also important to establish basic operating standards for how you conduct business. That means identifying values that you want to incentivize to achieve your goals and translating those values into an established norm or a code of conduct for how you engage and treat each other, your partners, and your customers.

These new operating standards will give you a stick against which you can measure how well you're meeting your goals. For example, you might establish that your organization values diversity of gender, race, ethnicity, and talent, as it is critical to developing broad viewpoints and serving diverse populations and customers. In the past, when measuring the success of a product or offering, you may not have considered how accessible it is to underserved and underrepresented communities. But now that you have reframed success to include that basic operating standard, you do.

When you reframe success by establishing new basic operating standards, you also are providing guidelines for how everyone in the organization can do well and contribute to accomplishing Jobs 1, 2, and 3. To continue the example above, a person on the customer help desk will be trained and incentivized to treat *all* callers with dignity and respond with compassion to the complexities of customers' lives. A product development team will be incentivized to consider partnerships that will enable underserved populations to access the products they create.

At HWCF, one of our basic operating standards was that everyone, regardless of economic level, would benefit from our efforts to reduce obesity. That was how we would measure our success. We were aware that wealthier Americans already could afford a wider variety of foods, enabling them to maintain a healthier diet. By committing to reduce the number of calories sold across their products (products at all price points), the HWCF companies created more affordable and healthier options for *all* families. In fact, our research later showed that our initiative reduced calories in every product made by the sixteen food and beverage companies, with only one exception.

The basic operating standards you set also will become the "ceiling of requirements" for how your partners will be expected to behave as well. When HWCF defined Job 1 as reducing the number of calories sold to make healthier foods more accessible to everyone, we incentivized all sixteen food manufacturers—our partners—to drive down cost and compete on taste and convenience to meet the needs of the largest number of customers. After all, while they had partnered on this venture, they were still market competitors.

Although standards must be meaningful, they also need to have a level of flexibility. Make sure your standards are broad enough that they are guidelines, not handcuffs. HWCF companies committed to reducing calories sold across their products within five years, but needed flexibility in how they made those reductions. We resisted setting strict standards—reduce fat calories by X amount or sugar calories by Y amount—since we were dealing with disparate products such as bread and ice cream, not to mention chocolate (which has a U.S. standard of identity with formulaic rules that allow the company to call the product "white chocolate" or "milk chocolate" and so on). Flexibility allowed us to meet our goal to reduce 1.5 trillion calories across all products and still measure up against our new success model to sell food products that tasted good at a price point any family could afford.

Besides setting new operating standards, you'll need to identify the metrics that you will use to measure whether you are successful. Here, the objectives and key results (OKR) methodology is invaluable. If you have never worked with OKRs, I encourage you to learn more about them. There are several books that can help you understand them and guide you on how to use them in your project or organization. The advantage of OKRs is that metrics defined to measure the success of a goal or an objective roll down and up the organization, from line workers to leadership. Everyone is incentivized to operate against the new metrics.

Finally, it's critical to change the terminology that you use to talk about success. Language helps motivate, empower, and energize people, keeping them committed to realizing your future. Language is also a signal for a transition in a market. You redefine success by giving it a new name. One of the best examples is the term *sustainability*. Once a word associated with environmental activists, sustainability is now an accepted Fortune 500 obligation, a metric of success that many companies have adopted. In corporate board rooms, we now talk about reducing carbon footprint and benefit-cost ratios related to environmental goals.

You, too, can establish a new nomenclature that sets the standard for how innovation is defined and success is measured in your area, market, or industry. These are the words you use to paint the future you want the world to embrace.

EVANGELIZE YOUR VISION

Once you've visualized the future, you have to bring everyone into the vision. You will be more effective speeding toward your goal if you don't have to battle people along the way. Get people to join you, stand down, or stand back by evangelizing your vision with care and tact. Focus on winning hearts and minds, and get people to buy into the future that you are visualizing.

As you recruit more people and partners to support your efforts, evangelizing your vision requires three strategies:

- Getting buy-in from as many people as possible
- Engaging new allies, including those who in the past might have been competitors or detractors
- Carefully building trust and relationships with those who will be affected by your actions

Getting Buy-In

To evangelize your vision, you need to ensure that people are buying what you are selling. Spending quality time getting as many people as possible to see how your vision will benefit all of you is well worth the effort.

To get buy-in, first you must identify the needs of every key player. Craft a document that outlines their needs clearly and shows where their needs and desires and your vision overlap or diverge. Then work closely with each party. To decrease adverse reactions to your vision, carefully and professionally walk through their concerns, acknowledge them, and get their opinion on how those concerns could be answered. See if they are willing to let go of their objections by showing them—through the use of facts and clear data—how your vision will allow them to achieve their objectives more quickly. In the process, you may need to compromise on a few points.

That's exactly what local businesswoman Sheila Johnson did when she set out to build a high-end resort, Salamander Inn, near my home. I live near a protected agriculture, Revolutionary-era village in Virginia that is known for actively blocking new development. Naturally, when Sheila proposed her new project, the town fought back. Residents feared that increased traffic and noise would diminish the serenity they and those in the surrounding countryside valued.

During the next few years, Sheila listened to residents' concerns and made a number of accommodations to respond to them. Most notably, she offered to redesign the ancient and faulty village sewer system as part of her build, an action that benefitted everyone—both her supporters and opponents. Sheila then could secure key allies and get the necessary permits to build the resort. By keeping her ears tuned in to the needs of her neighbors, she was ultimately able to reduce resistance to her vision. Today the Salamander Inn is a core part of our local social life.

Of course, Sheila was not able to get buy-in from every resident of the village, nor did she need to. And you probably can't convince every person of the benefits of your vision. Some people simply will refuse to buy into the changes you are outlining. If that's the case, quickly pivot to grow your universe of supporters so the naysayers become less relevant. When my then-tween daughter and her friends were excluded by the "cool but mean table" at school, the principal gave them wise advice. She suggested that they actively engage with other students to make their table twice as big, rendering the mean girls less relevant. No matter where you are in your life or career, this advice still applies.

As you work to increase the number of supporters, remember that you don't need to find people who share your exact viewpoint, and you don't need to surround yourself only with individuals who are over-the-top optimistic about your vision. Sometimes getting buy-in from pessimists and skeptics is even more rewarding. Not only will they constantly challenge your thinking, but if you are able to move them to your way of thinking about the future, the credibility of your vision will grow stronger.

You are not out to become best friends with every person. In fact, you may not even like some of them. Their personality or the way they approach problem-solving may rub you or your team the wrong way. Stay focused on getting agreement on the business goal, and above all, avoid creating a constant battle zone. My father always reminded me that you can't enter the future with someone shooting at you.

Engaging New Allies

If you are going to turn around your organization or project, you need allies. That's especially true if you are working in a project or group that is experiencing turmoil with others internally—or you are leading an organization that is at odds with advocacy groups or others in the industry (for example, the food and beverage manufacturers and the public health community). More allies are better than a few. Those who are opposing you or competing with you are busy building their own camp. You want to have a well-respected cohort by your side, supporting your new vision.

Here are some steps you can take:

- Identify the allies you need to publicly support your vision. Those allies might be peers or other organizational leaders. Assess them carefully—you want to be associated with people with a strong reputation for achieving similar objectives to those you are trying to accomplish. This will bring you credibility.

- If you are asking allies to support you and your vision publicly, you need to commit to protecting their credibility with their constituencies. This means being transparent and open with them when you communicate the changes you envision for your organization or project. Socialize these ideas with your core allies or ask for their input on how to communicate the new vision and ensuing changes. No one wants to be left holding the bag or taking the blame for endorsing changes that you are orchestrating without letting your allies know about them.

- Don't undercut your allies for short-term gain. Keep your eye out for any unintended consequences, such as hurting the allies' business or influence or cutting into an area that they see as valuable to their future. Focus on accommodating allies so you all can achieve the bigger objective.

The importance of enlisting allies, asking for their input, and watching out for unintended consequences is exemplified by the rise and fall of a vaping industry favorite, Juul.

For decades, everyone from consumers, to medical and public health officials, to government agencies has agreed that tobacco causes serious health risks. And yet one billion people around the world still smoke cigarettes.[3] A tobacco-free world certainly would be a perfect world scenario, leading to dramatic improvements in health.

In 2006, liquid nicotine vapes were introduced in the American and European markets. Right away, businesses[4] and investors saw an opportunity to solve what had seemed like an intractable problem and make this perfect world scenario finally happen. With e-cigarettes flooding the market, tobacco use declined, leading to positive health benefits for adults who previously smoked traditional cigarettes. The e-cigarette industry took off, and Juul became its most prominent player.

However, Juul was so enthusiastic about its product that it failed to get proper buy-in from the medical and public health communities and seek their input, resulting in unintended consequences. While studies suggest that e-cigarettes did provide a safe alternative for tobacco smokers who wanted to quit,[5] Juul's aggressive marketing tactics, including marketing fruit and candy-flavored e-cigarettes,[6] contributed to an epidemic of e-cigarette smoking among youths. Juul didn't take the time to form alliances with health professionals or concerned parents, to listen to their concerns, or to work with them on solutions.

As a result, the loud and influential opponents succeeded, and Juul faced a severe public backlash. By 2020, several states began restricting or prohibiting the sale of flavored e-cigarettes.[7] The big losers were traditional smokers, who were seeing positive health benefits from using e-cigarettes as an alternative to tobacco.[8]

Building Trust

To evangelize your future, you'll also need to build trust with your peers, employees, and allies inside and outside your organization. Building trust is never easy nor quick. It requires consistent due diligence in your dynamics and a fundamental shift in behavior as you develop a relationship over an extended period.

Maintaining trust and transparency is a hallmark of good leadership. After thirty-five-plus years orchestrating turnarounds, people I work with—inside and outside the organizations that hire me—know that I view our relationship as a lifetime relationship, not a transactional agreement to fix a problem. When you are done working with individuals on a project, they don't disappear. They go on to do other things, and in many cases you may need their partnership and alliance again. If you develop a reputation as a "one-off" transactional acquaintance, they might not be there the next time you need them.

Building trust among your allies and partners is also important. If you are new to the organization or project you are tasked with turning around, make sure that you understand the history behind any animosity that might exist among all parties involved. For example, underserved communities or key influencers may not trust some of your allies because years ago they took actions that negatively affected them. Or perhaps your organization under previous leadership undercut a partner that you are trying to recruit in a business deal. Or you discover that two of the key allies you need to work with have a personal rivalry that started when they worked for the same company years before—it turns out they haven't liked each other for twenty years! To move forward, you must restore trust between them. You might even serve as the trusted interface between them so they can slowly rebuild broken trust and broker a deal.

When I was leading the sixteen food and beverage companies of the Healthy Weight Commitment Foundation (HWCF) to achieve our vision—a meaningful cease-fire with the public health community by reducing the number of calories sold—it was clear that building trust was going to be critical. Our challenge was that we needed to sell our vision to those who had been most mistrustful of food and beverage manufacturers in the past.

We started by getting a leading, trusted name in the public health community, the Robert Wood Johnson Foundation (RWJF), to buy into our vision. After many conversations, they agreed to support the goal by serving as an independent outside evaluator of how well the HWCF companies met their commitment to reducing calories. While getting RWJF's support lent us credibility, working with us made RWJF a target. Many in public health were actually critical of *them* for negotiating with us!

No one had ever measured every calorie sold in America. There was no existing process for doing so. We were well aware that RWJF needed to maintain its credibility in the public health space, so we made sure to work with them on devising a high-quality, transparent process for measuring how well we achieved our goal. To serve as an independent judge of our efforts, RWJF ultimately decided to give the audit task to an academic public health leader, Dr. Barry Popkin, who was a harsh critic of the food industry. If the HWCF members were willing to subject their efforts to an analysis by the industry's biggest critic, then others agreed they would accept the audit results. Together, HWCF and RWJF worked to convince skeptics and critics that our commitment to reducing calories sold was sincere and that it would lead to measurable shifts in Americans' weight.

To do so, RWJF made the results of Dr. Popkin's audit publicly available. To build trust, we briefed the harshest critics of the food industry before every major announcement we made. This took shuttle diplomacy to a whole new level as our food and beverage member companies knew that at any time those critics might attack them and our process in the media. The good news is that they did not do so. People appreciated the efforts the HWCF team made to brief them. We showed respect for their work and listened to their points of view.

Most important, we built relationships of trust with them by acknowledging their concerns and recognizing they had many valid points. Our goal was to ensure that public health and policy makers could not only see themselves in the future we were building, but also trust that their goals were being realized through our efforts, albeit in a different way than they had imagined.

Investing in building trust from day one allowed HWCF to proactively demonstrate its willingness to "grow the tent," bringing more people and organizations into our success model. After securing the engagement of RWJF, the next key alliance we formed was with Michelle Obama's Let's Move! initiative, which sought to end childhood obesity within a generation. Following our announcement to collaborate with Let's Move, many health organizations and nonprofits contacted us, asking how they could work with us. HWCF invested in creating content that supported the core messages around healthy eating and exercise, as well as our commitment to reduce caloric consumption in the marketplace, which these organizations then distributed. We built an "active healthy lifestyles" evangelism strategy based on distributing digital content and open-source educational materials and building a coalition of the committed.

Ultimately, we were able to make meaningful changes to a public health crisis when the food industry had a seat at the public health table, and public health had a seat at the food industry's decision-making table. I have been pleased to see that those relationships have only grown more personal and stronger over the years as many of us are now able to work with each other to do good in other ways.

A VISION THAT BENEFITS EVERYONE

As you visualize the future, identify Job 1, reframe success, and evangelize your new vision, keep in mind that at every step you'll need to align incentives to deliver concrete change. You want to incentivize everyone involved in your turnaround to invest, work with you, and execute in a manner that supports the new future.

At the end of every process, you will be evaluating and reimagining as part of your turnaround people who have hopes and dreams. They have points of view they've arrived at based on their life experiences and ambitions. To make change, you need to motivate them. My father used to remind me that when redesigning reality, you have to tap back into the values people hold and the traditions they love. You must reframe their meaning within the world you are designing.

In January 2014, the Robert Wood Johnson Foundation announced that we had reduced 6.4 trillion calories in the marketplace[9]—beating our goal by 400 percent three years in advance. Later research by Dr. Bill Dietz, formerly of the Centers for Disease Control and Prevention, showed declines in obesity in certain socio-economic categories that aligned with our calorie reductions. During that time period, 99 percent of sales at the sixteen member companies were driven by these lower-calorie products, meaning the changes had been good not only for public health, but also for business.[10]

We never could have achieved this goal if the people within the parties involved had not been willing to put aside their interests and prejudices to devise a plan that met the goals of public health, government, and consumers. They took a risk, and it paid off for all. Change is always about people—leaders, employees, consumers, voters, partners, volunteers, and families. Your future vision will always have the greatest probability for success if it benefits people besides you, your project, or your organization.

The HWCF was an Apollo project that required a multi-million-dollar investment and a major shift across the food supply to turn around a seemingly intractable standoff between the food and beverage industry and the public health community. But you don't always have to take the moon shot to make a turnaround work. Sometimes a project that has a smaller scope or a shorter turnaround time might require a more modest approach. Regardless, the process is the same, and it always starts with visualizing where you want to end up.

Now that you have a clear vision for the future of your organization, project, or team, it's time to go back in time to examine what has worked in the past and, more important what hasn't.

STEP 2

BREAK DOWN
THE PAST

*Figure Out What Still Works and
What No Longer Does*

In June 2004, U.S. President George W. Bush and Japanese Prime Minister Junichiro Koizumi walked together on the beach at the Group of Eight Summit in Sea Island, Georgia. During the walk, President Bush reaffirmed a promise he had made to Prime Minister Koizumi a year earlier: that the United States would participate in the

2005 World Expo, which Japan was hosting in the Aichi Prefecture.

The World Expo, formerly known as the World's Fair, invites nations across the globe to present and display innovations in technology, architecture, and products. Each country stages impressive exhibition halls called pavilions, which run for as long as six months and welcome millions of visitors from around the world. More important, the Expo creates opportunities for countries to engage in cultural diplomacy and facilitate opportunities between trade partners and investors.[11]

Prime Minister Koizumi saw the Expo as an economic driver that would distinguish Japan on the world stage and reinforce its relationships with American business. Also, the Chinese would be hosting the next Expo, so U.S. participation in Expo Aichi would elevate our ally's position in this key region. Other countries were already well under way in building their experiential pavilions in Japan. The White House needed someone to take on the task ASAP, a position that carried the rank of U.S. ambassador.

I was honored when I was appointed to the role. The job sounded straightforward and the challenge tough but doable. I would have to raise private funding of $34 million from American businesses and get the pavilion up and running in just eighteen months. Time was so tight that I decided expediency topped formality. I drove to a Kinko's print-and-ship site, where a delighted notary put out tiny American flags and took my oath of office while customers and employees clapped. Glamorous? Not quite. Efficient? Yes.

After a formal ceremony at the State Department hosted by Secretary of State Colin Powell, I immediately headed off to Japan. That is where my dream job began to fall apart. As I drove to the airport, I received a call saying that the State Department was not allowed to pay for my flight to Tokyo to execute my official duties, which included signing a participation agreement with Japan on behalf of the U.S. government. They also couldn't pay for my two weeks of meals and accommodations. After accepting the job, I had discovered that I would not receive a salary, and I was expected to underwrite numerous flights to Japan and relocate my family for six months to one of the most expensive areas of the world.... What was going on?

When I returned to the U.S. after my initial two-week visit, Jim Ogul, a diplomatic employee who had been involved in a number of World's Fairs in the past, walked into my office and put down a couple of boxes. Politely and quietly, he said, "You need to read these." The boxes were filled with Inspector General reports of previous World's Expos. I learned that in the past 150 years, the United States had not been able to execute its participation in World's Fairs on budget.

In 1999, the *Washington Post* featured an Inspector General's audit that found questionable payments, employment of relatives, and overspending by the U.S. Commissioner General at the 1998 World Expo in Portugal. The overspending and implications of corruption, combined with a history of scandals associated with the World's Fair, were the last straw for lawmakers. Congress passed a law stating that no taxpayer funds could be used to support U.S. participation in future World Expos. I started to understand why the State Department wouldn't even pay for my trip!

The U.S. Pavilion needed to be ready to receive guests in Aichi. I had to quickly solve a complex problem that no one else had solved in 150 years, or the planned pavilion never would welcome a visitor. I had a few months to figure out why no one had been able to make the economics of World's Fairs work, raise the money necessary to participate in them, or manage the funds in a complex government system.

I started, as I always do, by visualizing the future for U.S. participation in the Expo. Happy pavilion visitors weren't my only end game. I wanted the Expo to create a tangible economic value that extended beyond it. I identified our core priorities:

- Job 1 was to cover the cost of the six-month Expo activities and exhibits while creating business and job opportunities for the United States.
- Job 2 was to create a spectacular event—even win "customer experience awards" (votes taken across visitors to the Expo)—in a cost-effective manner.
- Job 3 was to avoid inadvertently making a bureaucratic or financial misstep that would result in an Inspector General's report.

To deliver on Jobs 1, 2, and 3—that is, to make the future I had visualized a reality—I first had to go back in time. I needed to understand what about the design of U.S. participation in previous Expos was still working, and more important, what would get in the way of getting the job done and making the future I envisioned for it a reality.

No matter what turnaround you are managing, once you've visualized the future of the project, group, or organization you are transforming, you need to break down the past. You must examine the project's or organization's current assets—the products, services, programs, tools, processes, campaigns, etc.—and identify those pieces that no longer fit and those that are critical to filling any gaps.

All too often, we are brought in or find ourselves in a position to turn around a problem project that everyone knows is heading south, but no one seems able to articulate why. Instead, we say, "It's a mess" or "It's losing money." We can see the symptoms but haven't dug deep into the level of detail required to diagnose correctly what's wrong or to prescribe the right treatment.

Conducting an audit of a project's or organization's assets helps us do that. This is a time-consuming and thoughtful task. It is similar to dumping a box of jigsaw puzzle pieces on the dining room table, reviewing each piece, and figuring out whether it fits the picture on the box. At first glance, the pieces seem to work. For example, a service you offer might have a small but devoted set of customers. Your website might attract a steady set of visitors. The media make regular inquiries about what you are doing. Maybe your campaign seems to generate a good response.

But when you look closely at the puzzle piece, you realize that it might be the right color or shape, but it doesn't quite fit the picture you are trying to put together. When you dig deeper, you recognize that the number of devoted customers for that particular service has declined year after year, only a section of your website has attracted visitors, media inquiries have not led to influential coverage, and your campaigns have cost too much for what they bring in. These assets aren't working well, their costs outweigh their benefits, or they simply don't help to advance the new vision you have.

In this chapter, I'll walk you through the process for breaking down the past: conducting an audit of your assets; evaluating each piece of your puzzle, deciding whether it will help you accomplish Jobs 1, 2, and 3; and positioning your organization in the future you envision. I will help you decide what to toss and what to keep.

CONDUCT A THOROUGH AUDIT OF ALL ASSETS

To break down the past, you first must conduct a thorough audit of all the assets you are working with. Perhaps this seems like an unnecessary step. After all, you know the products, services, fundraising, and marketing campaigns in your organization or project inside and out.

But I'm asking you to go deeper. Identify all the *efforts* that your project, team, or group currently engages in. That can be a long list: Yes, it includes every product or service, campaign or program, as well as your processes (how you handle your sales); initiatives (what initiatives you make to reach a certain audience); external communication efforts (via websites, email lists, and social media); customer support (how you help your internal or external clients); and tools (what software keeps track of your products launch).

When I'm doing these audits, I find it easiest to get representative material of each asset—a brochure of a product, a sample marketing collateral or messaging, a printout of a software tool's main page—and place them in physical piles on a conference room table or my living room floor. The assets in each pile or bucket, as I like to call them, need not be of the same type—all your products don't have to be in a products bucket nor organized by where they live in the organization— all marketing-related assets don't need to go in a marketing bucket).

Instead, group the assets by the outcome they are involved in producing. For example, you might have a bucket of assets focused on attracting a particular type of customer. This bucket might contain advertising collateral, social media posts, and descriptions of customer service processes focused on that customer demographic.

While I like to spread out my piles of assets in a large conference room, you also can group assets digitally with an Excel spreadsheet or a Word table. Whether it's physical or digital, the idea is to create a visual of how your assets fit together. If there is a clear disconnect between an asset and your future vision, it will stand out like a puzzle piece that simply doesn't fit.

Not all pieces of the puzzle are easy to figure out. To make decisions about which assets to keep and deploy, you first need to critically assess their value: how well each asset will help you get Jobs 1, 2, and 3 done.

ASSESS THE VALUE OF EVERY ASSET

As I read the past Inspector General reports, I began to better understand the intricacies of the 150-year-old business model that previous teams had applied to managing the U.S. participation in World's Fairs. This business model resulted in a whole lot of fun for the people who were part of the experience, but a great deal of pain for national treasuries. I needed to do a deep assessment of the value of every single asset in my audit—every process, resource, activity, and program—that had been considered standard in previous World Expos. Just as I had to understand how well every asset of the previous World Expos supported our new vision, you will have to analyze the value of your assets and determine how well they support yours. You'll need to:

- Quantitatively rank and rate assets based on whether they generate revenue or expenses and on their cost inefficiency.
- Evaluate how the assets are perceived or valued internally *and* externally.
- Benchmark the performance of your assets against similar ones you consider best-of-class.

As you redesign and reimagine how to deploy your assets, understanding their true financial impact, their perceived value inside and outside the organization, and how well they stack up against the competition will help you decide what assets are worth keeping and which you need to ditch.

Assess the Financial Impact of Assets

All organizations, teams, and projects generate money to survive and grow. They exist because they *do* something for someone: A person benefits from an organization's service; the beneficiary gives it money. An internal team helps the sales department increase its sales; the CFO allocates more resources to it. Colleges provide services for students; they pay tuition. Government programs or advocacy groups provide services for certain communities: lawmakers or members of the public who value the impact to those communities fund them. Calling all this money revenue—whether it's derived from selling something or receiving from public funds or from a corporate budget—helps assign a quantitative value to everything you do.

Just as organizations and projects need revenue or money to pay their bills or grow, they also need to *deliver benefits*. Doing so costs money. The key is to deliver these benefits in a manner that is cost efficient—that is, in a way that takes into account the true or total cost of doing business. Often, in an effort to generate revenue, we spend so much money that it barely makes the effort worthwhile.

For example, many organizations or teams fall into the trap of overly customizing deliverables to meet the needs of their customers, clients, or donors. By doing so, they lose economies of scale and waste time, money, and resources. To get that business, they might do things that can't be duplicated or replicated, for example, a health and wellness program that requires individualized coaching. These become distractions as they redirect resources to inefficient processes instead of focusing them on the ultimate objective: a larger margin or less cost between making something and the cost for you selling it.

As you go through every asset in each of your buckets, you need to determine if it's revenue generating or an expense. If it's revenue generating, how effectively does it contribute to the current revenue stream? If it's an expense, how much does it cost, and how cost *inefficient* is it to fulfill or execute? Which assets have a more positive financial impact than others? Which expenses are the highest? Which assets are the most cost inefficient? Sometimes I find it helpful to rank each asset by assigning a numerical value of 1, 5, or 10—with 10 being the greatest value—to represent how critical the asset is in helping to bring my vision to fruition.

In the case of the U.S. Pavilion, I learned that previous Expo teams typically raised money from sponsors early in the process and used every single penny to pay upfront the hefty costs of building the exhibits. Then they had to go back and raise even more funds to pay for the cost of running, driving engagement, and fulfilling donor benefits at the Expo for six months. Of course, every previous leadership team had wanted their pavilion to be recognized as one of the top places to visit at their Expo. So they had gone way over budget to ensure theirs was the most innovative, technologically advanced, and engaging experience for visitors and VIPs.

As I audited what these Expo teams had done in the past—their fundraising processes, cultural programming, benefits provided to sponsors, accommodations and staffing, entertainment and dining packages, and so on—I asked: (1) How much did this cost in dollars and people's time in relation to value we got from it? (2) Will someone value the activity enough to sponsor it? (3) Will it have a tangible economic or diplomatic benefit that meets the objectives of our U.S. foreign and trade policies?

By assigning a quantitative value to each of these activities, I started to see a pattern. The issue was glaringly clear: In the past, the motivations behind the activities pursued were not necessarily aligned with the goals the United States had for its participation in the Expo—to create business and job opportunities for Americans. Instead, the motivation was to create the most engaging visitor experience. To avoid the issues they ran into, I identified ways we needed to redefine the cost model. For example, in the past Expos, the U.S. ambassador typically rented a local home to use for diplomatic events. Too expensive. Toss. Ambassadors also traditionally hired a military aide. Too complicated. Toss.

Evaluate How Assets Are Perceived within Your World

Every organization, team, or project operates in a defined context—a market, a business unit, a team, or an interest group—with some level of oversight from a board, an immediate boss, or key constituencies. The manner in which it executes its goals needs to resonate within those communities, which normally have a defined set of standards and norms.

As you audit your assets, you need to evaluate how they are perceived within the internal communities where you operate. How they are seen and perceived by others (Are they valued? Respected?) must be taken into account when deciding whether an asset will help you achieve your new goals. Is your marketing campaign seen as aligned with the rest of the organization's brand messaging? Are the products or services in your unit seen as important to your organization's bottom line? Are the processes you use to get things done respected?

I will never forget sitting in front of the Under Secretary of State and about twenty key government officials to discuss my plans for the Expo. At one point, an official kept going on and on about how past U.S. Commissioner Generals had held elaborate dinners, serving expensive wines. Could they trust me not to do so? I burst out laughing. I weighed barely over one hundred pounds. "Do I look like I eat lavish dinners and drink fine wines?" I said. "I just lost five pounds on the Tokyo trip because I don't eat!"

It might not have been my most dignified moment, but I got my point across. More important, this meeting clearly showed that these lavish dinners for sponsors—which had been fairly common, perhaps even expected, in previous Expos—were not only *not* valued internally at the State Department, but also were the source of deep mistrust. Those dinners might have served previous Expo teams to meet their goals, but they were not going to help me meet mine (especially Job 3!).

You also must also evaluate how assets are perceived *externally*—by customers, constituents, and partners. For example, as I audited the assets of previous Expo teams, it became clear that previous ambassadors had assigned the highest value to activities that focused on guest experience and entertainment. In some cases, they did not even realize they were doing so. Expos are similar to some extent to Disney World's Epcot. Guests visit different pavilions and enjoy experiences that can include rides, food, and "edutainment." Each country gets one day with access to Expo-owned entertainment properties, including the option of marching a parade down the main thoroughfare. It's easy to point your focus and efforts into creating the best experience for guests.

However, when I considered the activities that were most important to our host country and partner, Japan, it was clear that creating a great experience was important, but it wasn't the top priority. Dr. Shoichiro Toyoda, the honorary chair of the Toyota Motor Corporation and the honorary chair of the Expo, was using the event to elevate Japan and his company as key players on the world economic stage. The Japanese government knew the country's economic position would gain dominance if Toyota became #1 in global car sales. Toyota's Japanese partners and suppliers—from banks to computer designers and sound systems manufacturers—would all benefit.

While lavish dinners and an elaborate pavilion were fun, what our Japanese host and our American sponsors really wanted was to be part of the same business ecosystem. Our sponsors in particular wanted Japanese companies to build the supply chain in their home states as well as their car manufacturing sites. Everyone shared a common goal of economic development. Our assessment clearly showed that activities that prioritized opportunities in this area would be more valued and better perceived by our host country, potential partners, and sponsors.

Benchmark Assets against Competitors

Everything in business and philanthropy is a competition. You compete for limited dollars that may become even more constrained during a recession. You compete for people's time and attention. As you break down the present to evaluate what's working and what isn't, you also should consider how well your assets stack up against those of the competition.

Obviously, not every asset you've grouped in buckets can be benchmarked, but many—the services or products you offer, marketing or fundraising campaigns, customer service processes, etc.—can be. For these assets, ask the following critical questions: Is this activity or product or process just like everyone else's? Does it offer a unique value? Does it show off a valuable skill or expertise? Does it do something better than anyone else? Understanding which of your assets are best-in-class and which aren't will help you identify those that could help you realize your new vision.

When I was running the U.S. Pavilion at the Aichi Expo, one of the assets I had to benchmark was our entertainment and dining options for sponsors. As I've shared earlier in the book, we had determined that lavish dinners didn't help us achieve Job 1—to create business opportunities for the United States while covering the cost of running the Expo for six months in a cost-effective way. And they were not well-perceived by my peers in Washington. When we benchmarked the dining we offered our sponsors against what the best-in-class Expo country participants were offering, we realized that we were coming up short.

Since we could not compete against their customized entertainment options *and* contain costs in a predictable manner, we decided to change things up a bit. We turned to another best-in-class industry—high-end catering companies and luxury hotel experiences—and modeled our dining experience on them. We created three entertainment and menu options: gold, silver, and bronze. And staff delivered a gift basket filled with Japanese and Expo treats, as well as a personal note from me, to every sponsor. Our team made everyone feel special, but we added a level of predictability that allowed us to keep costs to a minimum.

My predecessors had focused on entertainment as their goal; I focused on creating long-term business relationships. When my team and I assessed the activities and programs of Expos past, it was evident that many of their activities did not align with our vision. This knowledge helped us make better decisions about what activities to cut and which to double down on.

KEEP OR TOSS: DECIDE WHAT STAYS AND WHAT MUST GO

Once you've made a comprehensive list of all the assets—the products, services, programs, tools, processes, campaigns, etc.—and have assessed their financial impact, how they are perceived internally and externally, and how they measure up against those from competitors, you need to identify which of these assets will help you achieve Jobs 1, 2, and 3 and which will get in your way.

To do so, classify each asset as:

1. Must-have—assets that will be critical to realizing your new vision
2. Nice-to-have—assets that align with your new vision, but are either too resource intensive or relatively more expensive than must-haves
3. Must-go—assets that are too expensive and cost inefficient, or simply don't help you achieve your new priorities (Jobs 1, 2, and 3)

Of course, deciding between the nice-to-haves and must-goes is not easy. Every project, group, or organization has at least a few assets to which people feel a strong attachment internally or externally. Perhaps some customers or constituents have great affection for a product or brand that has been around for a long time. Perhaps a program has value to someone internally with lots of influence over the process. Perhaps an important donor really loves a particular event, like the annual gala or summit. Your deep analysis and assessment of these assets, however, have revealed that they are problematic.

They might be cost ineffective or no longer fit with your vision of the future. But you are reluctant to disappoint your customers, constituents, or donors. You might think these assets can be saved.

Don't.

You can't keep inefficiencies or assets that dilute your effectiveness or the ability to realize your new future. If an asset does not allow you to increase your outputs while reducing costs, then you should let it go. Yes, everyone looks forward to dressing up and gathering for a gala, but if it redirects your staff's energy away from your true priorities, it might not be worth it...even if you lose your donor.

Sometimes it's tempting to hold on to an asset that no longer fits your vision simply because so much money and effort has been invested in making the asset fit in the first place. But if it doesn't work, you must cut your losses as quickly and painlessly as possible. That's what the Campbell Soup Company had to do. In 2012, it bought Bolthouse Farms, a specialized line of packaged fresh foods, in the hopes it would align naturally with its V8 juice healthier-for-you products. Only six years later, the company sold the product line. In a *Food Dive* 2019 interview, Jeff Dunn, CEO of Bolthouse, said, "It was probably just the wrong marriage. It just wasn't a natural fit. There was no synergy with the core Campbell's (shelf-stable) business, and it was an outlier."[12]

Of course, as you make decisions on what assets to keep and which to let go, write down any obligations you may have and find a way to extract yourself from them. These obligations might include legal or contractual obligations, such as to service a product or maintain a service for X number of years. I was once brought into a well-known company to help streamline their channel marketing program. Their salespeople were making too many exceptions to their standard contract as a special favor for clients. As a result, the company was managing 150 different licensing agreements in the same market. We quickly performed an audit; grouped agreements that had similar language; developed a streamlined, standard agreement that incorporated the majority of benefits; and then transitioned everyone to the new norm.

In nonprofits or corporate social responsibility programs, the obligations often can be inferred based on the organization's history with a specific group or community. For example, a company or nonprofit may have always given money to a particular charity. However, as the organization changes, it might realize it needs to be more strategic to have a greater impact and focus on other communities in a bigger way.

Whether an asset that no longer works carries an obligation, legal or an inferred, the key is to establish a clear end-of-life date, giving the affected parties time to adjust. It's often painful to face the reality that your project, team, or organization has been propping up an inefficient asset or program. But as a leader, you must be transparent, clear, and diplomatic when announcing these kinds of changes. For instance, to continue the example of the gala event, you might announce that you are putting the event to "sleep for a while" but plan to bring it back in the future in a new, more sustainable, and cost-effective form.

REASSURE EMPLOYEES, PARTNERS, CUSTOMERS, AND YOUR COMMUNITY

As you make decisions about what assets to keep and which to let go, it's important to understand how these choices affect others and how they are perceived by employees, partners, customers, and the community.

Change brings anxiety. People feel bounced around as their reality shifts, and uncertainty grows. They become cynical and wary. They are fearful about maintaining their livelihood or losing a project that made them love their job. Any party with a vested interest in your project's, team's, or organization's success will need to trust that the tough, sometimes draconian decisions you're making will truly lead to a better future.

When I accepted my assignment at Aichi Expo, I knew our Japanese host team was nervous about whether we would show up at all! Our involvement in previous World Expos had been rocky. Secretary of State Colin Powell had to pull out from the German 2000 World Expo just two months before it opened due to a lack of funds.[13] As China grew ever larger as an economic and military leader in the region, Japan needed the United States publicly by its side, committed to a mutually beneficial economic relationship. Dr. Toyoda was already expanding Toyota's investments in the U.S., but he needed us to bring together investors and suppliers so the two countries could engage in more business together. They had a lot at stake.

As I assessed and tossed activities that no longer served our future vision for how we would participate in the Expo—especially drastic cuts in entertainment and dining that had become expected from America in the past—I had to be aware of how these actions might be interpreted (i.e., that perhaps the United States didn't care or wasn't invested in the Expo). So while I cut assets and costs, I had to build trust and credibility with our host country and other Expo participants.

My best and least expensive asset in this endeavor turned out to be me. My personal time became the essence of high-touch diplomatic engagement delivered at no cost and in a manner that provided value and long-term benefit. Our family visited other country pavilions and met with key diplomatic and business contacts. My six-year-old daughter drew pictures and sent thank-you notes that endeared her to all. (I would later see her drawings hung on the walls of ambassadors' offices and in the homes of Japanese CEOs.) I consulted with leaders, including the president of New Zealand and a prince of Saudi Arabia who wanted to understand how we had successfully privatized U.S. engagement at a World Expo *and* managed costs. Most important, if I got an invitation to visit a village, I went—even if it meant sitting in a small fishing boat in my St. John suit and heels at twilight. My team focused

on consistency at every touch point. We weren't transactional, but relationship driven.

Above all, building trust requires:

- Acting with transparency. If you were brought
  into the organization to lead a turnaround, do
  not hide your plan. When you are making decisions about what assets to keep and what has
  to go, be prepared to talk openly about the
  changes and why they are necessary.
- Leading with numbers. When communicating
  about the assets you'll need to abandon, focus
  on the financials. Numbers do not lie and often
  speak for themselves.
- Being direct. Once you've identified an asset
  that needs to go—say, an expensive program that
  no longer delivers as much value as it used to—
  rip the bandage off. Don't let people build false
  hopes that the asset can be saved.

When you are in the process of breaking down the
past, your employees, partners, and others vested in the
success of your organization or project might be appre-
hensive. If that is the case, meet them where they are at
and think about what is important to them. They don't

need flashy, expensive dinners. Write the thank-you note immediately. Return phone calls. Reassure your employees with one-on-one meetings. People want to know you respect and value them.

BREAK DOWN THE PAST WITH COMPASSION AND HUMILITY

The Aichi Expo closed on September 25, 2005, after six exhausting but rewarding months.

Job 1 was done: We operated the U.S. participation at Expo on budget, with 100 percent non-federal funding while facilitating opportunities for American businesses.

Job 2 was done: We exceeded our attendance goals and were twice rated the #1 pavilion by visitors (competing with nearly two hundred nations). We also received extensive international and Japanese press coverage.

Job 3 was done: We avoided bureaucratic or financial missteps and instead were recognized on the floor of the U.S. Senate as a positive fiduciary model.

Dr. Toyoda said at a closing innovation summit, "This Expo could not have been a success without U.S. participation." By breaking down the past, we were able to change course and avoid the mistakes of our Expo predecessors. We also were able to identify the assets that would give us the most bang for our buck. But more important, laying all the pieces of the puzzle on the table and discarding those that didn't fit exposed the empty holes, giving us a clearer sense of the pieces needed to complete our beautiful picture. In the next chapter, we'll talk about how to find these pieces and how to put them into play.

CREATE A PATH FROM PRESENT TO FUTURE

Map Out Critical Decisions and Actions Needed

In 2018, Food Allergy Research & Education (FARE), the leading national organization working on behalf of the eighty-five million Americans affected by food allergies, was struggling financially. Although FARE had been the beneficiary of a sizable financial reserve due to the generosity of donors, it was on track to use it up within three years unless changes were made. The organization also had an adversarial relationship with the food and beverage industry, and research into the disease was about fifteen years behind that of other diseases. The food allergy space did not have a sustainable infrastructure that would advance solutions quickly.

When they hired me to be their new CEO, I asked the FARE board to envision the organization's perfect future scenario. What would they want the food allergy space to look like in five years? They wanted FARE to be at the center of positive change, coordinating buy-in from all the parties—government, food and beverage industry, patients, medical researchers, and other large nonprofits—on a strategic plan of action. In this vision, everyone had a seat at the table and was focused on a common goal: to find treatments and therapies that reduced the risks associated with food allergies and prevented the rise of the disease.

I went straight to work. When I dug deep, it was clear that supporting and funding transformational research using one of our most unique assets, the FARE Clinical Network, was our special sauce, our core competency. The FARE Clinical Network sites are a coalition of top food allergy medical centers around the country, led and coordinated by FARE, that provide state-of-the-art care and treatment for food allergy patients as well as conduct research. If we could get the money to scale up collaborative research and data sharing among the centers in our network sites, we would be able to differentiate ourselves clearly from others in the food allergy space and have a bigger impact.

To get there, we needed to get the following done: Job 1 was financial; we needed to raise $200 million to accelerate research. Job 2 was creating a collaborative business model; critical partnerships would be key to growing exponentially as they would allow us to align spending, share resources, and co-fundraise when there was mutual benefit. Job 3 was funding transformational research supported by clinical and research data collected from the FARE Clinical Network and beyond. These priorities were at the center of our five-year strategy.

I worked with a small leadership team to audit all our assets, grouping into buckets everything we did, from our programs and campaigns to the informational content we published for patients. After benchmarking our assets against those of best-of-class organizations such as the Crohn's & Colitis Foundation (CCF) and the Juvenile Diabetes Research Foundation (JDRF), we were able to identify several activities that took significant time and resources but did not align directly with our new vision. Among them were some fundraising activities such as walkathons. These cost about two million dollars to raise about one million dollars! They got the grass roots engaged but did not make enough money to cover their costs or invest in research. In fact, we found that many of our resources were focused on unsustainable activities, and we unfortunately had to get rid of them.

We were now ready to see how we could best deploy the remaining assets and programs to get Jobs 1, 2, and 3 done. We were committed to expanding our research infrastructure to build scale and revenue streams that would fund and support our research. Now we needed to figure out how. We evaluated the pipeline of potential therapies that would be coming into the market and identified the gaps. We prioritized making big bets on patient data acquisition along with funding therapies and diagnostics that were accessible and available to all patients. We also placed patients' voices at the center of every decision. We listened to them and their families as they shared the effect the disease had on their daily lives. We heard the fear and anxiety that parents felt when their children went to school or summer camps. Based on these conversations, we knew we had to support innovative therapies for children and young adults that were not complex, but easier for patients to manage in their busy lives.

For eighteen months, we researched and redesigned our organization, resulting in a massive restructure. The most invaluable tool to help us get there was our "decision tree"—a visual snapshot of how the pieces worked together that helped guide strategic decisions at all levels. It allowed us to up-level our capabilities and sunset obligations that were no longer relevant or required as we moved on to new operational standards.

In the previous chapter, we explored how to audit your assets (products, services, programs, tools, processes, campaigns, etc.), identify which align with your new vision and which don't, and toss any that no longer fit. Now it's time to decide how you will use your remaining assets and evaluate whether they can perform at the levels needed to get Jobs 1, 2, and 3 done. This requires making critical decisions about where to invest resources, what to promote, and what is your baseline requirement to operate.

While you may have a clear picture of these assets and their moving parts, your team members who focus on keeping the fires burning and the trains running on time while you are out evangelizing your new vision may not. You need to systematically bring them along on the journey, helping them understand the role the assets play and giving them clear direction on how to move forward.

A decision tree is a visual tool that helps you and your team make decisions about the remaining assets and lets everyone see clearly the assets that you don't have and that need to be developed to reach your goals. They also help you determine where to allocate your most valuable resource—your people—and where those people might no longer be needed. As you move from restructuring your team to realizing your perfect world scenario, decision trees create alignment across your project or organization so everyone is on the same page. They provide a path from the present to the future.

CREATE A DECISION TREE

A decision tree is essentially a flow chart, a yes/no visualization process I learned when I worked at Intel many years ago. The idea is to group the assets you were left with after your audit in categories and run them through three essential questions. Each question forces you to answer "yes" or "no." The answers help you: (1) Make decisions about which categories to pursue more strongly.

(2) Determine which assets have the most potential to provide value and where you should invest the most resources. (3) Identify opportunities where you can extend the value or revenue generation of an asset. As you answer these questions, your new business framework will begin to emerge.

Here's how to create a decision tree, step by step. You can see what a completed decision tree looks like in Figure 3.1.

Step 1: Group Assets in Categories

The first step to building a decision tree involves grouping your remaining assets once more. This time, however, you will group assets that are alike. Some typical categories for your groupings include products (all products, services, and offerings); media and marketing exposure (your logo, website, promotional campaign, etc.); and joint ventures (your partnerships).

Next, identify the target market and the size of that market for each asset. At FARE, our asset categories fell into three buckets: (1) research (our patient registry, the FARE Clinical Network); (2) education (starter kit for newly diagnosed patients, webinars, our college program); and (3) advocacy (many studies, including a National Academy of Sciences study and another on frequency of hospitalizations due to anaphylaxis). Once you've identified the categories and listed the corresponding assets under each, start asking the following questions.

Step 2: Does the Asset Meet Baseline Requirements Needed to Compete?

Understand where you are now with each asset and what investment levels are required for you to own the space they operate in. In addition, determine whether your assets meet baseline operational needs, that is, to support the day-to-day tasks necessary to carry out the basic activities of your project or organization. As you are accelerating toward your new vision, you still need to meet these baseline requirements and customer obligations to get your product or offering out the door.

At FARE, the baseline requirement was providing basic support and education for the food allergy community. For example, we know students are more at risk in their teens and in college because they are more likely to engage in risky behaviors such as not carrying their epinephrine autoinjector or dining at places that don't manage issues of cross contact well. Our FARE Teen Advisory

Group and the FARE College Program were assets that met our baseline requirements, one by raising awareness of these important issues among teenagers, the other by raising awareness among college students and providing technical assistance to food service companies so they can better manage allergens when cooking.

Step 3: Does the Asset Continue to Be Cost Effective?

As you consider the goals for your project or organization (Jobs 1, 2, and 3), you'll find that some assets that survived the first round of audits will accelerate you toward your future, while others will not. The ones that don't might look less attractive as you perform deeper cost-benefit analysis. Start by analyzing whether each asset can operate at the baseline performance level. Then determine if your operational prowess will enable you to set new strategic growth opportunities.

At FARE, our educational content was best-of-class, but the way it was delivered allowed us to serve only a small group of families. The products were good but too expensive and time-consuming to deliver. For example, we had a popular "newly diagnosed kit" that doctors gave to families after a child tested positive for food allergies. The kit gave parents a snapshot of the most important information. It was a comprehensive resource, filled with medical information, tips, door hangers, and kid activities. However, it was extremely expensive to print and mail. It was also bulky—one could imagine a parent struggling with stuffing the large package in a diaper bag while dealing with children and strollers. The content was important, so we had to find a new way to deliver the information cost effectively. In the end, we solved that issue by directing parents of newly diagnosed patients to the FARE website and later to an app where the information in the original kit is delivered in a set of videos.

Step 4: Can You or Should You Add a New Capability or New Feature to Existing Assets?

As you create your decision tree, you may determine that by rearranging or building out your assets by partnering with another organization, team, or project, you can introduce a new capability or asset that significantly increases either the revenue or impact of your project or organization and allows you to realize your vision more quickly.

However, sometimes we get excited thinking we've added a new capability, when in reality we've just added a new feature or benefit to an asset. To make sure you avoid this mistake, pick apart your assumptions: Analyze the core of what you are doing to determine if you are truly creating a new asset that provides a new product, service, or value—or if you are just improving the original asset or providing the same value or service in a different way.

At FARE, we had many discussions about creating an app to make our educational and medical resources more accessible to busy families. We saw the app as a new capability giving families access to "evidence-based food allergy resources right from their pockets." We were so focused on the app that we failed to recognize it was only an interface that allowed patients to engage with FARE in even bigger ways than they had before. The app was not the end game, but rather a piece or new feature of our evolving capability of providing information to our community and gathering vital clinical data for our researchers and industry partners.

Step 5: Is the Asset a Market Differentiator?

In each category, consider whether the asset is expected to generate significantly greater revenue or value than the cost of branding and marketing it. If it is, you have an opportunity to make several strategic moves, from extending your offerings or brand to differentiating certain product lines as premium ones.

At FARE, the Teal Pumpkin Project during Halloween is a high-performing niche campaign. A Teal Pumpkin on someone's doorstep signals that a house is giving out non-food treats (toys, trinkets), in addition to candy, so children with food allergies can safely trick-or-treat there. This seasonal campaign was extremely popular, driving the highest engagement numbers for the FARE website as well as extensive media attention. When we were doing our decision tree, we saw the popularity and effectiveness of this short campaign and realized we could extend it into a Teal Holidays series that enabled us to engage families year-round. Holidays cause great anxiety for food allergy patients because they often can't eat many of the traditional foods served at family gatherings. Our goal with the expanded Teal Holiday series was to create awareness of how to make family members feel safe and included during times of the year when food is often the focus.

As you evaluate your assets against your core competency, you may realize that certain ones should be considered premium assets, deserving of more resources. In other cases, you may subdivide key parts of your project or organization to provide clarity on which assets have a premium value over others. For example, at FARE, we identified research as our core competency. It soon became clear that the FARE Clinical Network was our premier asset as it not only drives dollars through investments made by donors into critical research, but also is at the heart of our collaboration with patients and researchers. The decision tree helped us clearly see that to achieve Jobs 1, 2, and 3, we needed to make it stronger. We rebuilt the program, dividing the medical clinics in the network into three groups based on clearly defined capabilities: transformational research, clinical trials, and standards of care. In two years, we grew the network from thirty to fifty clinics and turned much of the network's focus on collecting patient data and sharing that data among researchers.

The exercise of creating a decision tree will help you home in on your top assets. As you do, you'll have to keep tossing those that are nice-to-haves but not necessary to fulfilling your perfect future scenario. Getting rid of nice-to-have assets is difficult—after all, there is nothing particularly wrong with them. Many may provide value

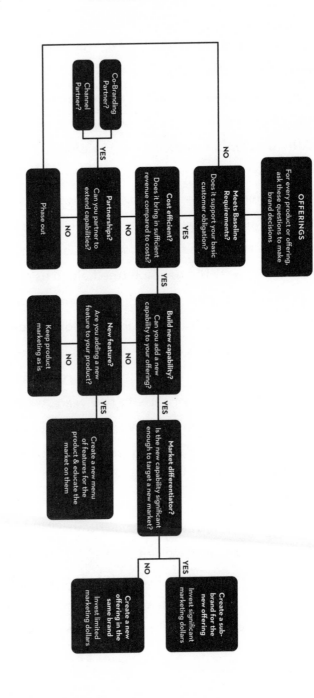

FIGURE 3.1 SAMPLE DECISION TREE

and probably have for a long time, so there might be an emotional attachment to them.

More important, whenever your cut assets—whether they are must-goes cut during the auditing phase or nice-to-haves cut during the decision tree phase—you often have to make another set of heart-wrenching decisions: determining who in your team has the business experience that will be needed in this new business framework and who does not.

BUILD THE RIGHT TEAM TO EXECUTE YOUR DECISION TREE

Once your decision tree is done, and you have a path to the future, you need to determine whether your organization is ready and able to execute it. You must assess whether you have the right people to do the job, enter the future vision with you, and mature with the organization. I find that whenever I've turned around an organization or department, building the right team happens over three phases: (1) the initial restructuring, (2) the first performance review cycle, and (3) attrition.

The Initial Restructuring

At the earliest stages of a turnaround, you probably will experience churn—people leaving in quick succession—for a period of time. It's an unavoidable process in the transformation journey. Some people will leave on their own as they realize that their skills or interests do not align with the new vision for your project or organization. However, you will need to part ways with others as their roles are tied to assets that no longer support your new vision, or their skills are not suited for the new assets and capabilities you are developing. Even if you re-train teammates whose positions are no longer needed, a few well-meaning individuals simply won't have the technical skill set or willingness to learn new capabilities.

Above all, to pull off a turnaround, you'll need to work with people who are on board with your vision as well as comfortable with change. It's imperative that you root out teammates who are neither. I call them "bad apples" and "bad bananas." In my decades of doing turnarounds, I've found them in most organizations.

Bad apples are people who are loath to make the changes you've proposed. They may oppose your new vision in an effort to preserve the old ways of doing things or the old mission of your project or organization. They might even inspire others to join them in standing against change. My advice is to offer them a good deal that reflects their tenure and influence in the community and negotiate them out the door with dignity and respect. If you gently walk these people out the door, you may be able to preserve a few others in the group and repurpose their skill sets.

More problematic are the "bad bananas." These are people who might be excellent individual performers, but who have an overall negative attitude. They spread negativity until others are disgruntled, too. Even if they are not directly in the fruit bowl, they often cause the other fruit to go bad. You must address their behavior head on—some may not even realize that their negative attitude has an impact on others—or let them go. Otherwise, your organization or project will not be able to move forward with the positive energy it needs.

If you are lucky, you will find plenty of team members champing at the bit to try new ways of working and approaching the mission of your project or organization. They will thrive in your change environment. That's what I found at FARE, where I worked with members of our education team who were thrilled to partner with national organizations such as the Girl Scouts, registered dietitian organizations, and school nurses—something that FARE hadn't done before. They were excited to work closely with new people, extend the reach of their content, and try new forms of distribution. These are the people you want to retain, train, and support. They have the potential to thrive, serve as a bridge between the old and new, *and* help you realize your new vision.

During this initial phase, you must be transparent while retaining a human touch any time you communicate restructuring decisions to your team. It is important to remind anyone on your team that your decisions have a direct impact on people's livelihoods, families, and personal reputations. Compassion and empathy are critical, as is a level of professionalism. You must show respect for the dignity of the individual. Treating people with respect is not only a human resource requirement (you could face legal action if someone is treated poorly), but also a *human* requirement. How you treat people as they depart reflects on you not only as a leader, but also as a person.

That's a lesson I was reminded of in 2017, when John Medica, tech turnaround guru and friend, unexpectedly died at age fifty-eight. John was known as the guy Michael

Dell recruited from Apple to turn around the Dell laptop business in 1993. But above all, he was known for his character. As my husband and I attended an event celebrating his life, I was not surprised that much of it centered on his leadership style. His friend Mark Vena wrote in a *Forbes* article: "Upon reflection, what I remember most about John is not his accomplishments in the technology space at Dell (which were enormous), but the plain fact that he was just a kind and good person."[14] I don't know about you, but being an effective, good, and kind person is how I, too, would like to be remembered.

How you want to show up as a leader and a person is worth considering when you have been brought in to manage a turnaround. Walk in the door ready to acknowledge that you have been tasked with restructuring the project or an organization, and that this will inevitably lead to people leaving the organization. When you meet with your team members to share this, speak with facts. Briefly outline—without disparagement or emotion—the business reason that requires a restructuring, such as loss of revenue, risk to reputation, or a toxic culture. Explain to team members the steps you will take to begin the process, including the audit of the current assets and the decision tree.

If you know that people must be let go, let them know as soon as possible. As you lay out your vision for a new future, team members will begin to worry about their jobs. They'll have conversations with their peers in hushed voices and speculate whether there's room for them in your new vision. On my first day at FARE, I held an organization-wide meeting to let team members know right away that we would be conducting a reduction-in-force, also known as RIF, in the next ninety days. I wanted to be honest with them so employees would know what to expect and not have to guess behind closed doors.

When you communicate that there will be a restructuring, it's important that you convey the following:

1. We will be respectful of every person. If someone's position is eliminated, it's likely because of market dynamics or a result of a change in the priorities of the organization or project—not due to issues around competence.
2. If someone's job is cut, we will provide them with support. We value their service and want them to continue to have a successful career.
3. To make this turnaround work, we need employees who are flexible and have a positive attitude.

4. While we know going through a restructuring is hard, we must continue meeting our customers' or constituents' needs—they deserve that.

My advice is to tighten the timetable for this restructuring as much as you can. If you treat people with dignity and support them well on their way out, ripping off the bandage as quickly as possible is often less painful for everyone involved.

The First Performance Review Cycle

Following the initial restructuring, it is essential to give the remaining team members a chance to succeed and show you what they can do. They are likely feeling shaken since their friends just left. They are concerned they will be next. By offering them training or retraining opportunities, you will give them the best chance to prove that they can help accelerate your vision and therefore earn a place in it.

Assign mentors to the remaining team members so they feel supported and have the resources to shift their skills and focus onto the new priorities. More important, share with them the rules of the game. Ensure that every person understands the new vision, and rally everyone around Jobs 1, 2, and 3. Reframe the definition of success as described in the first chapter. Team members need to understand that success will be measured using different standards. Set explicit goals and objectives for them and align them with Jobs 1, 2, and 3. Establish performance measurements that are quantitative and tie compensation, bonuses, and promotions to both team members' performance and their work's impact on the project's or organization's goals. Give them a heads-up that their performance will be evaluated in the next review cycle.

After the initial restructuring at FARE, our team established goals and performance measurements for the remaining staff. We introduced new language that reframed the success of our organization and every individual within the context of revenue—money raised to fund our mission—and helped people understand the assets that were cost inefficient. People knew it was time to lean in if they wanted to be part of the long-term vision.

Six months later, we had our first performance review cycle since the initial restructuring. As part of our commitment to transparency, we had acknowledged to employees that performance reviews would guide the next phase of restructuring. I held another organization-wide meeting to explain how staff would be ranked and rated for both their performance and their impact on reaching our goals.

Even when you offer the best professional development and mentorship to your team members, some might not transition successfully to a new role after their original job is eliminated or improve their performance to operate at the higher levels needed to pull a turnaround. But other team members might surprise you; people who might have been flying under the radar in the past will shine given clear direction. Their skills and talents might not have been a perfect fit or might have been undervalued or deemed unnecessary in the past, but they are a perfect fit for the vision you are trying to build.

When you identify these star performers, incentivize them to stay. As your organization or project up-levels its reputation or standing externally in the marketplace or internally in an organization, your star employees will become more competitive in the marketplace as well. Retaining them should be a key priority.

Attrition

In the months that follow the initial restructuring and the first cycle of performance reviews, talented people may decide to leave on their own. Perhaps they see fewer opportunities for themselves within your new structure. Maybe the asset they are working on (a campaign, product, project, etc.) used to be a bigger priority than it is now. Or maybe they are not in their comfort zone when the project or organization is changing. Sometimes despite your best efforts and theirs, even the most can-do spirit may not be a good fit with your new vision, and people may decide to move on to something new.

When people notify you that they are leaving, focus on creating a positive departure experience. Offer to write a recommendation letter for them or post a positive recommendation on their LinkedIn profile. Thank them for their service in an email to the whole group or at a meeting. Take the time to acknowledge the good things they've done. Celebrate their success: They deserve to be recognized. Plus, you never know when or how you might find an opportunity to work together again.

As you untangle yourself from the relationship, do it in a way that you can re-engage with them when your goals align again. If they leave for the competition, stay friends. You may become fierce but ethical competitors, so collegiality is a must. You never know when your worlds will intersect down the road. Whenever someone departs, I remind my staff that the world is small. As I have gotten older, I have learned that inevitably you will meet these individuals again. This is as true in the tech world as it is in Washington, D.C., where people move frequently from job to job. So always manage relationships carefully. It is easier to meet people as old friends than as enemies you created by how you handled their leaving.

Don't forget that leaders need to take care of themselves, too. Even if you are resolved in your actions, creating a decision tree and rebuilding your team to execute it is a tough and emotional process. Sometimes you may have self-doubts or feel sad as people you like decide to leave or can't achieve their goals. Throughout the first few weeks of the turnaround, set up a thirty-minute end-of-day call with a mentor or the person who hired you.

In my early days at FARE, I talked with Dave Bunning, the board chair, at five o'clock every evening. During that call, I listened to his advice on how to handle difficult situations, expressed my frustration or angst in the "cone of silence," and pressure-tested my ideas for how I would resolve a problem. It was my moment to be human and vulnerable. We continue to have our frank discussions, but they have become less frequent and more focused on urgent business topics.

Finally, never forget that you have an external audience to communicate with and reassure as to the stability of your project or organization while you restructure.

Keep customers, partners, donors, or investors in the loop. No one wants to be surprised. After more than thirty years turning around organizations, I have learned that details always come out. Whatever you do, don't try to hide anything. Own your story and tell it with a focus on where you plan to take the organization.

CONTINUOUSLY REFINE YOUR DECISION TREE

At this stage, you have a decision tree guiding the strategic moves you must make to get Jobs 1, 2, and 3 done. You also have a strong team in place to bring your future perfect scenario to reality. Your team gradually will transition from coping in the midst of radical change all the time to operating the day-to-day business normally again. For example, you will not be constantly restructuring your team, but rather people will start moving across, up, and down (and out) of the organization in the course of the regular cycle of employee performance evaluations.

If you are orchestrating a turnaround that will take several months or years, it's possible that changes in your world and the world at large—a new technology, a business model, a new public policy change, a shift in leadership within your parent organization—may present an opportunity for you to refine your special sauce or core competency, making your organization truly unique and a bigger player in its space. Also, as your project or organization begins to turn around and emerge into a leadership position, it will receive attention. Other departments or leading organizations might see an alignment between your interests and theirs and approach you about partnering. Success breeds success.

However, success also requires embracing constant change and innovation. As Andy Grove, former CEO of Intel, warned us, "only the paranoid survive."[15] There is always a competitor waiting in the wings to knock you off course. So you need to be agile and committed to a process of continuous improvement. The steps that you've taken thus far to achieve your vision might turn out to be just a bridge to an even brighter future than you anticipated.

As you start moving in the right direction, it's critical that you pause to engage in a new audit of your assets and to further refine your decision tree. Now that you've increased your capabilities, are there any opportunities to improve or scale some of your assets or make them even more cost effective? For example, a new technology might allow you to deploy an asset more quickly and increase your reach. Or you've been introduced to another organization or department whose interests align with yours and might allow both of you to accelerate your growth or effectiveness.

As FARE started meeting its goals in the primary areas of focus, our success brought us to the attention of bigger industry players in a variety of sectors. Our access to patient data—which we had worked hard to scale—was valuable to them and would accelerate their ability to provide patients with a wider array of treatments and information. That, in turn, allowed us to continue growing and scaling our operations to meet our goals.

When you benchmark your assets in this new audit, remember that you might need to compare them against new competitors. When you benchmarked your assets initially, you were doing so against your best-in-class peers. For example, if you are a nonprofit focused on reducing the use of tobacco, in the first audit you might have benchmarked your assets against those of other nonprofits focused on smoking cessation. In this next round, you want to benchmark against larger leaders in adjacent spaces (for example, bigger nonprofits that focus on a cause such as heart disease). Benchmarking against the next level of competitors will help you up your game.

Auditing your assets and subsequently refining your decision tree might lead you to sunset more assets and reshuffle your team as you align internal resources to meet your enhanced goals. This is likely to ruffle some feathers. Remember to carefully roll out the next stage of your vision in a manner that allows everyone—your team members, leadership, partners, donors, and investors—to see that you are evolving, not going in a new direction.

Reframing success in a way that internal and external partners and critics understand how your vision is taking shape and evolving is something you'll have to do constantly, just like auditing your assets and refining your decision trees. This focus on continuous improvement will allow you to realize your future and grow far beyond it.

At FARE, our decision trees guided us through making critical choices about what programs to keep and where to refocus our resources. Within eighteen months, we had restructured the organization by 83 percent. By the end of 2019, the FARE team had increased revenue (donations) by 62 percent while keeping expenses relatively flat. We reduced our overhead by 30 percent and fundraising expenses by 10 percent—resulting in a profit increase of a resounding 676 percent. By the end of 2020, we had received more than $85 million in financial commitments against our $200 million goal. We also had grown our FARE Clinical Network by 60 percent, which allowed us to collaborate with patients and researchers to grow the clinical data needed to support major research. We are making significant progress toward getting Jobs 1, 2, and 3 done.

More recently, as our vision has started to come into focus, we've continued to reimagine that future perfect scenario and expand those it includes. Building on the diversification of FARE's leadership and boards, our team launched a multi-sector diversity, equity, inclusion, and access (DEIA) program to ensure access to care and therapies for underserved and underrepresented communities and elevate their voices as decisions are made.

As I write this book, the world is still reeling from the unprecedented economic and social impact of COVID-19. By following a disciplined decision-making process combined with stringent cost management, FARE thrived in 2020 even as many organizations struggled. Despite the pandemic's challenges, we were able to continue making an enormous impact, increasing our commitment to research, education, advocacy, and awareness of food allergy.

You don't need a pandemic or some other challenge to catch you off guard and derail your turnaround. In the next chapter, we'll explore how you can execute your turnaround plan to ensure success.

EXECUTE WITH SPEED, CONFIDENCE, AND HEART

Set Aggressive Goals and Foster Effective Partnerships

Nothing gets me more energized than visualizing a better future for an organization or a group and persuading people to run up the hill with me. I thrive in that sense of "we" versus "me." I can see us reaching the top together, backslapping, whooping, and heading to a bar to reminisce about where we started and where we find ourselves. When I get to the top, my joy comes not just from reaching the big goal, but from celebrating that success with those who got there with me. Together, we own that success.

I'm lucky to have experienced that sense of satisfaction many times in my career, especially in the three turnarounds that I have shared with you throughout this book. At the Healthy Weight Commitment Foundation, we reduced calories in the marketplace to ensure that healthier foods were accessible to everyone in the United States. At the Aichi World Expo, we managed to raise the funds necessary to cover the cost of American participation while facilitating business opportunities between the United States and foreign investors and trade partners. And at FARE, we restructured the organization by 83 percent in eighteen months to create a sustainable research infrastructure.

In all three of these aggressive turnarounds, I ran fast, ran hard, and tried to stay as agile as possible. During a turnaround, I live in a constant state of paranoia, assuming that competitors are ready to pounce at any moment. I learned to adopt this paranoid mentality in my first post-government role at Intel Corporation. Andy Grove, Intel's CEO, believed "that change can mean an opportunity to rise to new heights. But it may just as likely signal the beginning of the end."[16] In the midst of a turnaround, I'm fully aware that if I am not able to quickly move an organization, a project, or a team to a higher level of performance, we will lose the advantages we've gained by going through the hard exercises of defining Jobs 1, 2, and 3, aligning our assets around them, and crafting a strategic plan to realize our new vision.

Competitors will always be at your heels, ready to catch up to you. Being slightly better than them is not going to cut it anymore. Otherwise you'll find yourself in a perpetual game of cat and mouse with your competition. That's why you need to run. Really fast.

Once you have a plan for how to best deploy your assets and move forward, you need to quickly and confidently execute your turnaround strategy. If you take too long debating your executional path, you will lose. Three tools will help you move with speed and agility: setting aggressive goals, partnering with others, and leading with confidence and diplomacy.

SET AGGRESSIVE GOALS

To pull off a successful turnaround, you need to be willing and brave enough to set audacious goals. In the first chapter, we talked about setting the priorities of

Jobs 1, 2, and 3 that will allow you to bring your future perfect scenario to fruition. The decision trees that you created in the previous chapter will help you identify the moves and investments you need to make to get these jobs done.

But to succeed, you'll also need to set Big Hairy Audacious Goals (BHAGs) for each of these jobs. Introduced by Jim Collins and Jerry Porras in their best-selling book *Built to Last*, BHAGs are long-term goals designed to get everyone energized to meet a target that is clear and exciting.[17] The goals themselves don't need to be audacious on the world stage. They just need to be bold in the context of your project, program, or organization. A sales manager's goal might be to increase her team's revenue by 50 percent. A community leader might commit to building a coalition to reduce hunger in her zip code. A school might set a goal to improve testing results of a particular at-risk student group. The key is committing to transformation.

To successfully set aggressive goals against your Jobs 1, 2, and 3, you must make them quantitative and public, inspire everyone in your team and beyond to achieve them, and constantly communicate progress against them. Let's take a look at each of these requirements.

Set Clear, Quantitative Goals—
and Make Them Public

For three decades, I've learned that to leap through inflection points, you need to set clearly articulated, measurable goals. The first step to setting these audacious goals is to decide the impact you want to have with your Jobs 1, 2, and 3, determine what it will take to make significant progress toward them, and set a clear quantitative target.

Here's a simple but clear example: If you are turning around a failing sales team, your Job 1 might be straightforward: Increase sales while decreasing cost per customer. You might decide that to do this, you'll need to expand the categories of potential customers from your traditional customer base to two new segments, the scope and impact. The aggressive goal you set is to increase sales by 30 percent in six months, with 15 percent coming from customers in a new segment.

The only way you are going to hold yourself accountable for your goals is if others know about them. So publicly commit to them. Be transparent about your goals with your team, your bosses, and your external stakeholders. Talk about them whenever you can so your target stays front and center in everyone's mind.

If you are inside an organization or a company, make sure to set a goal that makes your boss sit up and notice. You want people to go "wow." If you are an organization competing in a particular sector—academia, business, government—set goals that will move others to readjust their targets to compete with *you*. That competition is what changes the environment. No one wants to be the only team or division in a company without a coherent and aggressive goal.

Setting aggressive quantitative goals becomes trickier when the impact you want to have cannot be quantified as easily. Sometimes, for example, your Job 1 might be to have an impact on people's behavior. You may want your customers or constituents to improve a skill or become healthier or start caring about something. If that's the case, first you'll need to determine what it would take to fundamentally change the reality of the total population that is affected by your offering or by the byproduct of your actions. Then you'll have to decide what impact you could have on this population within the context of *what you own* and find a way to measure that.

For example, when in 2009 I became the head of the Healthy Weight Commitment Foundation (HWCF), a coalition of sixteen beverage and food companies determined to help solve the problem of obesity, I had the CEOs' commitment to launch an Apollo project (see the first chapter). The Job 1 necessary to make this future a reality was to reduce the number of calories sold in the United States. Our companies owned the intake of food as they produced 35 percent of the food and beverage products sold in America. While we couldn't own the entire problem—after all, Americans still ate at restaurants and cooked food at home—we could reduce the number of calories sold within our market parameters by changing the recipe of existing products, introducing lower-calorie package sizes, and launching new lower-calorie products.

Public health scientists, doctors, and epidemiologists had determined that a reduction of 100 to 140 calories in daily consumption would allow an individual to maintain or reduce weight. So we calculated how many calories we would need to reduce across all products sold by our companies in a five-year period in order to make that happen. In May 2010, we announced our goal with First Lady Michelle Obama at the White House: We committed to reducing 1.5 *trillion* calories across all products sold by our sixteen companies in five years. Now *that* got people's attention.

Get Everyone Excited about Reaching the Target

When you set aggressive quantitative goals, it's critical that you get everyone in your team onboard and excited about meeting them. Going after audacious goals can be intimidating. How you communicate your goals and substantiate their importance makes all the difference.

Your job is not only to get teammates to buy into these goals, but also to strongly commit to them. You must get them to see themselves as a unit, working together to reach this target. Help your teammates integrate these audacious goals into their own objectives so that their collaboration and their results clearly ladder up.

OKRs, or objectives and key results, are a helpful goal-setting methodology that can help you do that. Created by Andy Grove at Intel and most recently popularized by John Doerr in the book Measure What Matters, OKRs track and measure each person's actions against measurable goals.[18] If your goals are clearly stated, you can align them with individual teammates' OKRs to ensure that everyone is working in unison to meet them.

You also have to inspire your team to meet these goals by creating momentum through shared optimism, focus, and resilience. If your goals are clearly stated and align with those of your project or organization, even periods of setback can make your team more inspired to drive forward. Success is not instantaneous, but by golly, you are going to get there as a group.

Make sure you get everyone—not just your team-mates—excited about your audacious goals. Today more than ever, we are called to create not only value for our projects, programs, and organizations, but well beyond them. Organizations, in particular, are expected to create economic value not just for themselves and their share-holders, but for the economic benefit of the community. In 2019, the CEOs of Business Roundtable, a nonprofit dedicated to promoting business and public policy, committed to lead their companies for the benefit of *all* stakeholders—customers, employees, suppliers, commu-nities, and shareholders. Setting audacious goals that get all these stakeholders invested in meeting them is key.

An example of a company that has done so success-fully is Nestlé. The food and beverage company operates its businesses grounded in well-defined global goals to "create shared values." It leads with concrete actions and big numbers, as is clear from the three main goals listed on its website:

- For **individuals and families**, to help fifty million children lead healthier lives.

- For our **communities**, to improve thirty million livelihoods in communities directly connected to our business activities.

- For the **planet**, to strive for zero environmental impact in our operations. [19]

Like many other Fortune 500 companies, Nestlé knows that when competition is creeping into your space, aggressive, well-defined goals are required to revitalize and focus each team member and beyond.

Communicate Progress to All Stakeholders

As a child, I used to participate in our church's fundraisers. I loved looking at the simple red "thermometer" constructed of paper that showed how well we were doing against our goal. It always inspired me and others to push harder and fill the thermometer with red, all the way to the top.

Tracking the progress you and your teammates are making toward your goals not only motivates you to do your best, but also alerts you when you've stalled and need to correct course. It's also critical that you report your progress regularly to your bosses, the board, donors, investors, or constituents. Keep all decision makers informed of the positive leaps you've made to reach your goal as well as any barriers you've hit.

As you report your progress to those above you, remember that they are busy people. Show clearly through quantitative measurements how your team is performing against its audacious goals. If you are transparent, you will be able to bring everyone along in the turnaround journey with you. And they all will feel a sense of accomplishment when you succeed.

If you are an organization that is facing outside criticism—you are hoping to turn it around after having a PR crisis or facing regulatory or legislative challenges—you might consider identifying an independent outside evaluator that not only will validate your goal and the methodology you are using to achieve it, but also can evaluate the progress you are making against goals. Getting such an independent evaluation will lend credibility to your efforts and restore trust if needed.

Before we announced our giant goal to reduce 1.5 trillion calories in the marketplace by 2015, we needed to find someone with credibility in the public health space to act as an independent outside evaluator of how well we had met our goals. The Robert Wood Johnson Foundation, a premier philanthropic organization focused on health issues, agreed to do so. In 2014, after a thorough analysis, they publicly confirmed that the sixteen Healthy Weight food and beverage manufacturers reduced 6.4 trillion calories in the marketplace by the end of 2012, exceeding our original goal by 400 percent three years in advance.

Setting aggressive goals can accelerate your turnaround. However, they can be especially tough on you, the leader, who has to inspire and motivate everyone to reach for what at times seems like an impossible target. Sometimes when I am struggling, I get inspired by re-watching my favorite sports turnaround movies, the ones where the coach sees the potential in the athletes and takes them to victory. One of my favorites is *Miracle*, featuring Kurt Russell as coach Herb Brooks, who led the U.S. men's hockey team from a humiliating early game to victory against the Russian team and the gold medal in the 1980 Olympics.

If you find yourself discouraged, get your inspiration wherever you can—a book or a movie—and keep at it. You may have to run up that hill a few times as you discover new boulders on the road that need to be removed. But never give up on the goal if you can afford to make it happen.

LOOK FOR OPPORTUNITIES TO PARTNER

Great turnaround leaders know that you don't reach a major milestone on your own. No one person, team, or organization has the capacity to do everything. If you are leading the turnaround of a project within your company, you might need to partner with other departments or peers outside your group. If you are an organization, you might need to partner with another one to reach a bigger audience.

A good partner often can help you move more quickly by (1) providing a capability that you need but is too expensive to develop or acquire on your own; (2) helping you reach a market, a customer base, or a set of constituents that you don't currently have access to; (3) being better at executing in one of the areas that is not a core competency of yours. The right partnerships also can help you reduce expenses. More than that, they can help you build credibility with new audiences that don't know you but are familiar with your partner.

The key to a good partnership is to identify partners who are willing to align their objectives with yours to achieve a common outcome. Partnerships were at the heart of the turnaround of America's participation in the 2005 Aichi World Expo. As I shared in the second chapter, the United States participated in past World's Fairs (as they were known) at the government's expense. The U.S. created and funded the programming completely on its own, a cost-ineffective model that resulted in it pulling out of the previous 2000 Expo in Hanover, Germany.

When I was appointed to lead the United States' participation in the Aichi Expo, my team and I had to find private funding for the traditional cultural programs and exhibits that characterize the six-month event. In addition, I had to fund activities that facilitated business meetings among U.S. companies, state governments, international investors, and trade partners.

As we looked for partners, we considered the economic interests of both the United States and the host country, Japan. Toyota was building momentum to become the #1 car company in the world. Japanese companies were looking to set up manufacturing operations overseas in markets in which they were selling and building the supply chain required to support Toyota's car production.

With that in mind, we reached out to state governments to partner with us. American governors and economic development teams very much wanted these Japanese companies to set up shop in their states. Their tourism boards also wanted to attract Asian tourists with deep pockets to their cities and vacation spots. Since their interests aligned with ours—facilitating introductions to the right international business contacts—they helped fund the business development programming at the Expo.

These state governments also had economic development budgets that allowed them to bring artistic talent to Japan, while also helping us fund our cultural programming. We also partnered with large American companies with global footprints. For example, media companies such as Warner Brothers and Sesame Street saw Japan and other Asian countries as significant markets. We were able to partner with them to leverage a movie release or some other media campaign in ways that benefited the U.S. presence at the Expo.

The engagement at the Expo was a resounding success from financial and consumer standpoints, as our partners worked closely to drive foreign direct investment and tourism dollars between the United States and Japan. We did this not by focusing on ourselves, but by spreading the success broadly and sharing credit with our partners.

Partnerships like the ones we forged to meet our goals at the Aichi World Expo can help you accelerate your own future perfect scenario. But not all partnerships are the same, and figuring out what to look for in a partnership requires careful consideration.

Partnerships Come in Many Forms

If you are considering a partner to execute your strategic turnaround plan, it's important to understand the various kinds of partnerships. What all have in common is that they involve two or more entities joining to help each other meet their aligned goals. The terms for these partnerships sometimes are used loosely, and there are differences among the parameters of each of these forms. I recommend focusing on the outcomes that each produce, particularly if you are not in a Fortune 500 setting and are just trying to figure out how to partner with others in your small team, community, school, church, etc. Here are the most common types of partnerships:

Co-Branding or *Co-Marketing Partnerships*

These partnerships allow two or more companies to market products together. Sometimes organizations join forces to play off their name recognition and expand their markets. J.M. Smucker Company and Kellogg's did just that when they co-branded Pop-Tarts filled with Smucker jams, each brand hoping to attract the other's consumer base.

These partnerships are especially helpful when consumer companies and nonprofit groups partner for a common good. When I served on the board of Girl Scouts of the USA, I was part of the team that worked on forging a partnership with Nestlé to co-brand Girl Scout cookies with its coffee creamers. The Girl Scouts received a revenue stream from the sale of those products, and Nestlé benefited from being associated with a renowned charity and its mission to empower girls.

Many small organizations are attracted to co-branding partnerships as a means to grow their reach. I have watched many an eager marketer and partnership program manager get excited about the number of organizations that want to partner with them. But they often fail to look closely at the size of the audience those organizations bring. Always investigate what a potential co-branding partner can offer.

Almost always, you'll be better off focusing on a few excellent, top-tier partners with the largest audience rather than with multiple smaller players.

Channel Partnerships

When you partner with someone to help you sell or distribute your products or offerings, you are joining forces with a channel partner. Channel partnerships grant you access to new distribution capacity that would be too expensive to create yourself. A channel partner typically has an established user base, membership, or active community that can extend the reach of your content or offering.

For smaller organizations and groups, especially nonprofits, channel partners can be key drivers of growth. Smaller groups and nonprofits have limited budgets, so they must find novel and inexpensive ways to deliver value to their constituents or customers. Through channel partnerships, nonprofits can increase the capacity they require for growth while the channel partner benefits from being associated with the mission of these nonprofits.

I have relied on channel partnerships to build capacity for many nonprofit programs I've been involved with during the years. I have partnered with the Girl Scouts, the National Association of School Nurses, and the Academy of Nutrition and Dietetics for the distribution of health and wellness curriculum and food allergy awareness content.

Public-Private Partnerships

These partnerships align your company's or organization's goals with those of governmental or quasi-governmental programs. Public-private partnerships offer large organizations the opportunity to practice business diplomacy, promote public policy that serves their interests and communities, and facilitate economic growth and success. For example, Dr. Derek Yach, a former PepsiCo senior vice president, created a trilateral partnership involving the United States Agency for International Development, the United Nations World Food Program, and PepsiCo. This public-private partnership sought to build long-term economic stability for small chickpea farmers in Ethiopia by helping them increase their crop output and source their product to PepsiCo's supply chain.[20]

Corporate Social Responsibility Partnerships

These partnerships allow you to align with organizations with societal impact. Coca-Cola and the World Wildlife Fund, for example, partnered on the protection of polar bears in the Arctic Circle as a brand campaign for Coke, built around our affection for these playful North American creatures.[21] Corporate social responsibility partners can help you achieve your corporate social responsibility goals and increase your brand presence by leveraging their unique value add.

Regardless of what type of partnership you chose to pursue, finding the *right* partner will be the key to accelerating your turnaround.

How to Find the Right Partner

The ability to build strong, trust-based partnerships has defined every turnaround in which I have been engaged. Picking the right partner is crucial. After all, partnerships require a long-term, stable commitment, and these commitments are often tied to expense. Before you engage in a partnership, make sure that you are a good fit. This is what to look for.

A Partner Who Will Offer a Capability You Don't Have

When choosing a partner, consider what is unique about your organization or project and what you excel at. Look for partners who can help you meet any capabilities that you are missing to accelerate your goals.

A Sophisticated, Mature Partner

As you select your partner, consider who is best-in-class in the areas where you need help. If you need help with distribution, find the partner with the broadest, most engaged user base or community. The more established and sophisticated you partner is, the less of your time they will require. They know how to do what they do really well and probably know how to partner with others. Small partners tend to absorb more of your time, and your growth may be held back by the limitations of their reach or lack of prowess. Of course, be realistic about whether you are in a position in the marketplace to interest a top partner contender. If you are a start-up or small organization or project with a unique capability, you need to be creative to get a bigger player to work with you.

A Partner with a Compatible Operational Style

A successful partner operates at the same level of sophistication as you do and is interested in creating shared value. You want a partner who is responsive, can see the big picture, has a similar process-oriented approach, and shares your vision of the future. You don't want a partner that becomes enmeshed in bureaucratic details. Instead, partners should share your attention to detail while keeping their focus on the ultimate goal. If they begin to micromanage and become adamant about using their specific methodology for every task, take note of it. Micromanaging and demanding constant readjustments signals that your goals are not aligned.

As you consider the right partner for your organization, remember the most important of criteria: Your interests and goals must align.

Partner in Unusual Ways

Sometimes you might not be able to find a partner that meets all the criteria above. There are exceptions to every rule. For example, you may discover that a larger player is too bureaucratic, and you will be more successful working with a smaller, nimbler, and more innovative partner. You might share a common, get-it-done attitude with this smaller partner, but have dissimilar styles of execution.

Other times, you may need to align with a partner with whom you have significant differences—whether it be the way they approach business or, more common in the nonprofit world, what their policy stance is.

Having a common goal, similar attitude, and agility may be enough to align. But you must set this unusual partnership up for success:

- Recognize and acknowledge your different operating styles and the issues on which you agree and disagree.
- Coach your team on how to mitigate the challenges that your stylistic operating differences present.
- Don't get pulled into your partner's drama. My sister-in-law often repeats a wise saying: "Not my monkey, not my circus." Partnerships give you a snapshot of another team's or organization's internal workings—and they are not always pretty.

Sometimes you won't have a choice except to join forces with unusual partners. Sometimes you will need them more than they need you. If that's the case, remind yourself and your team of your organization's place in the value chain and respect what the partnership contributes to your end goal. No one said that alignments would always be easy.

How to Make Your Partnerships Successful

President Ronald Reagan kept a sign on his desk that read "There is no limit to the amount of good you can do if you don't care who gets the credit." This is particularly true for partnerships. The best partners can move quickly when everyone involved leaves their egos behind and focuses on meeting their shared goals.

When I joined FARE, the largest private funder of food allergy research, members of the food allergy community were engaged in acrimonious infighting. (See the third chapter.) The community was small and not expanding in an inclusive way. The board wanted me to quickly foster positive collaboration with government, the food and beverage industry, patients, and other large nonprofits to provide education, drive advocacy, and identify treatments. One of our first goals was to create a collaborative culture within FARE and the broader food allergy community. One of the ways we did that was by creating positive incentives for organizations, especially in the food and beverage industry, to want to partner with us.

Recognizing their priorities, we helped them understand the size of our community. We partnered with McKinsey & Company on a research project that revealed eighty-five million Americans did not buy foods containing the top nine proteins that can trigger allergic reactions due to food allergies and intolerances. At the same time, we worked with Global Strategies Group to survey families who are dependent on governmental supplemental nutrition assistance. With this qualitative research, FARE was able to demonstrate struggling families' need for access to affordable products that are safe for them. We also used this research to show food and beverage companies that food allergy families constitute a lucrative and loyal customer base for them.

To have a fruitful partnership, you need to understand your partners' needs and find common ground. This isn't always easy, but it works. Here are some ways to ensure that your partnership succeeds and helps you meet your goals.

Be Generous in Your Relationships

Instead of asking, "What can you do for me?," ask "How can I help?" Generosity of spirit goes a long way. Make it a point to understand what your partners need to be successful and outline what actions you can take to meet their end goals. Perhaps you can remove obstacles or open new doors for them. Sometimes it is as easy as serving as a reference for your partners' program, inviting them to attend your event for free and giving them a spotlight moment, or reposting one of their big wins on your social media sites. Acknowledging them is a win-win, as everyone will see your commitment to the success of those helping you.

Being generous in your relationships also means demonstrating through your investment in the partnership that your team or organization is willing to sustain the relationship for the long haul. You are asking them to invest heavily in the partnership, so you need to invest your time, people, and other resources, too.

Be a Committed Partner, but Set Clear Boundaries

While you should show your partners that you are in it with them for the long term, you also must manage expectations by clearly stating what you can deliver for the partnership and what you can't. Build a document to outline your shared goals and a specific list of each other's requirements of participation. When the opportunity presents itself to do something special beyond your agreed-upon goals, then go for it. It doesn't have to be big. I have found many an opportunity to refer partners to a speaking engagement or include them in a media interview that highlighted the partner's unique offerings.

Celebrate Collective Wins

It does not matter whether you are in a big or small organization: You can always foster support by giving your partners credit for their role in achieving results. Or you can award a collective win to all partners involved in performance reviews, town hall meetings, press releases, and the like. At FARE, we use our communication platforms to recognize our partners. Through our newsletters, annual impact reports, presentations, and digital platforms, we highlight partners and collaborators outside of our organization.

See the World from the Partner's Point of View

If you have partnered with an organization or a team whose opinions fundamentally diverge from yours, it's important to listen to them. Understand what they care about. Couch your language in their vocabulary to show your respect for their position. And use my 60/40 rule:

If you agree with someone 60 percent of the time, trust that you can agree to set aside the 40 percent you disagree with and find a path forward. Focus on the areas where you agree today, and place issues you disagree on in the parking lot for future discussion.

When I led the Healthy Weight Committee Foundation representing sixteen food and beverage companies, my team and I partnered with public health organizations and leaders who believed that consuming many of our companies' products led to poor health outcomes. It wasn't always easy, but we were able to align interests around our common goals—reducing calories—and put our differences aside.

Don't Move So Fast You Leave Your Partner in the Dust

Sometimes you're moving so fast toward your goal that you look around and discover you've lost your partner on the way. If they can't move as quickly as you need them to, talk to them. See if you can revisit the partnership parameters until they have emerged from whatever is holding them back.

When the COVID-19 pandemic hit, we saw this problem emerge a lot at FARE. Smaller partners were overwhelmed as employees were out of the office or transitioning to digital workspaces, requiring them to put key programs on hold. Keep moving forward to meet your goals, but be respectful and transparent while you outline an alternative path forward with them. Treat the existing relationship with respect even as the partner struggles. When that partner is back on its feet or experiences a turnaround, your relationship will be even stronger because you cared for them. If you have the power to pick someone up, then help shoulder their burden and keep advancing. It is the most important thing to remember when you move quickly.

Don't Take Yourself Too Seriously

In the early 1900s, my husband's great-uncle painted a portrait depicting a wizard and a man peering at the writing of an ancient tome. Underneath the painting, there's a plaque with the following words: "'This,' said the Ancient, 'is the most important precept of them all'—and bending forward the successful man read in letters of gold, 'Don't take yourself too damned seriously.'"

You may represent a large entity or an important team or project within your organization, but you are "you" no matter who pays your paycheck. Don't overestimate your importance. Treat everyone and every partner with equal respect. Do not take credit when it does not matter. Let go of something that may not be important to you but means a great deal to your partner. By doing so, you will move more quickly as people will applaud your progress instead of form alliances against you in response to your bad behavior.

Focus on collaboration and show a willingness to subjugate your own ego in order to serve your members, customers, or community. When I'm working with a team in the nonprofit sector, I remind my team that our job is to support the goals of those who fund us. When we face critical budget decisions, we remind ourselves that it's not our money, it's the donors' or sometimes our partners' financial investments. Political battles and wars of words are not about us, our egos, or our professional goals. The focus is the end game of the organization or team we serve.

LEAD WITH CONFIDENCE AND DIPLOMACY

When you set aggressive goals and partner with others to execute your turnaround strategy as quickly as possible, you are bound to hit some bumps along the road. You will be learning as you go, so there will be situations where you inadvertently make mistakes. When that happens, recognize your mistakes and own them.

EXECUTE WITH SPEED, CONFIDENCE, AND HEART

I learned the art of managing mistakes well when I studied Chinese in Taiwan in 1989. Maintaining relationships is a critical part of the Chinese culture, so it's not surprising that there are many different Chinese phrases to express an apology, depending on the situation. Some apology phrases are used if you are saying sorry for actions that made you lose face, while others are used if your actions caused someone *else* to lose face. The idea that your actions might lead you to lose face or cause someone else to be embarrassed is an effective way to reframe a situation and see it from the other person's point of view. Acknowledging the impact your actions had—either inadvertently or because of poor execution—on another party may eventually get them back to the table.

This is the time when it is critical to be transparent. When you make a mistake, let your boss and other necessary stakeholders know, and lay out the actions you'll take to address them. Mature businesspeople know that some things go south, but will appreciate your transparency. Sacrifice a bit of your ego because a leader needs to be willing to take the hits in order to move everyone beyond the immediate problem.

The art of diplomacy—gentle nudging, looking for avenues to move another party to "yes"—is critical to moving quickly and nimbly. It's also exhausting. Creating and maintaining goodwill means never letting your guard down and always displaying a positive presence despite any personal frustrations you might be feeling. I fully admit that sometimes I go home, turn to my husband and say, "I am so tired of having to be nice to everyone." But I know that the next morning I will dust myself off and jump in the car or on a plane to visit the next disgruntled party.

Throughout it all, you need to remain firm while you smile and be gracious. If you have followed the method outlined in the book, trust yourself and your decisions. Don't constantly revisit them. You have made tough calls, but the organization or project is in dire straits, so they must be made.

To move forward confidently, avoid some of these common pitfalls:

- **Perfectionism.** Don't let perfect be the enemy of the good. Nothing is perfect. Use your decision trees to help you make the most viable, sustainable move in that moment. As you come out of your turnaround, you will have plenty of opportunities to reassess and perfect.
- **Consensus.** It's important to have enough

supporters on your side to execute your strategy. However, once you bring an issue to the table, talk about it, and make a decision on it, do not reopen the discussion. Stand firm, knowing that you followed your decision tree, and move on. At Intel, where I worked early in my career, they use the phrase "disagree and commit." This means you can have direct, sometimes argumentative conversations and disagreement, but once a decision is made, everyone, including the dissenters, gets on board.

- **Blinders.** Sometimes it's difficult to see value in what others have done or hear a different point of view. To see value, follow my 60/40 rule, which I explained a few pages earlier. Acknowledge the good things proposed by another team member, a critic, or a key stakeholder. Identify the common denominator which you can agree on as the measurement of success.

- **Opportunism.** As you execute with speed and desperately need to show progress, it is tempting to go for the quick or opportunistic win. But don't sacrifice a sustainable solution for a short-term win.

Above all, remember that if you run so fast that you end up running over the interests of others in the process, no one will like you by the time you get to the end goal. Your success will not last long as others will become more invested in seeing you fail as opposed to succeed.

Great executives with whom I have worked left their egos behind and reached out to others to help them achieve success. They used a personal touch to show others they genuinely care and to maintain meaningful relationships. They never feel too important to take time to pick up the phone or make an introduction.

Many years ago, I was touched when JP Bilbrey, then Hershey's CEO and a member of the Healthy Weight Commitment Foundation board, called me from Beijing to tell me how proud he was of me. He was reading the *Wall Street Journal* while having breakfast and came across a story about me mentoring high-performing employees. Heidi Roizen, a Silicon Valley venture capitalist and powerhouse, is known for her willingness to connect people and support their endeavors. An avid writer and speaker, she provides encouraging words publicly and privately, especially to female entrepreneurs in the tech world. The late Fred Malek, former president of Marriott Hotels and chair of Northwest

EXECUTE WITH SPEED, CONFIDENCE, AND HEART

Airlines, continued to send me a note or call years after we worked together whenever he saw a news story highlighting one of my programs.

These personal touches mean a lot. They encourage people to keep going, especially when things are tough. So as you speed to your future perfect scenario, make sure you stay grounded and show gratitude for everyone who helps you in the journey. It will help you pull off your turnround today and many more in the future.

CONCLUSION

End on a High Note

You did it! You followed the four main steps outlined in the book—visualized the future, audited your assets, created decision trees, and executed with speed, confidence, and heart. If you remained steadfast to this process-oriented approach, your turnaround should be complete or nearly so. Your once-failing project, team, or organization finally is stabilizing.

In the process, you turned skeptics and critics into enthusiastic supporters. They value your transparency and trust the quantitative metrics you used to track your progress and results. Team members, peers, and partners are vested in the long-term success of the turnaround, as you made sure to share the credit with them. And your project, team, or organization is probably being recognized—either within your company or out in the market—for its unique core competency.

But the future today will not be the future of tomorrow. Your success is likely to attract the attention of competitors. They'll be nipping at your heels. That's why you can't rest on your laurels—your project, team, or organization needs to evolve continuously. Although you're done with your turnaround, I encourage you to periodically repeat the processes of auditing your assets, ranking and rating them, and tossing what no longer works. Revise your decision trees and continue to set aggressive goals to expand your influence across your organization or broader market.

It's also time to make personal decisions about your role. You took up the mantle of leadership when things began to go south. It is likely that your ego or identity is wrapped up in the success of your turnaround. After all, the future vision that you worked so hard to make a reality is highly associated with *you*—you brought it to life. Now your vision is embedded within the project, team, or organization, and it's the standard way that it operates.

The question is: Should you continue your leadership role through the next phase of growth, or is it time to go? The decision is not always easy. The turnaround has become your baby, and it's hard to let go, but sometimes you have to if you want to end on a high note.

EXTENDING YOUR STAY

When you visualized the future at the beginning of the process, I encouraged you to set a milestone and an end date by which you hope to turn around your project, team, or organization. I always recommend setting timelines because they drive performance, encourage you to execute with speed, and force you to make hard decisions that you might delay unnecessarily without the pressure of a deadline.

In my career, I've had the honor to work in government positions serving an elected official. When you work in that environment, you know you have a set number of years (in my case, four years) to execute your vision before the next election cycle. If you are lucky, you might have more. But your legacy probably will be tied to the first years, when you were getting the most important things done as fast as you could.

Once that timeline is met, you might decide that you want to see how your turnaround fares in the next phase of its life. If your goal was to turn around a project or team within an organization, you might decide you want to stay at the helm and keep continuously improving the outcomes and results. If your mandate was to turn around an entire organization, big or small, you might feel that you have a vested interest in seeing the organization grow and transform long-term.

When deciding whether to extend your stay, it is important to recognize your preferences and limitations. Leaders come in different packages. Some are turnaround queens and kings who thrive when operating in perpetual change. They are motivated by personal fulfillment when they succeed where others have not.

I will admit that I am such a person. I can put my heart and soul into a turnaround and suffer through the exhaustion and the hits, because in the end I know I have worked with others to create a sustainable organization. In the introduction, I shared the story of how, when I worked at Intel, I was involved in helping to build a school in Chandler, Arizona. That was a deeply satisfying experience, and every year, I check in on the school to find out whether it still ranks in the top ten schools in Arizona. I love turning around organizations, programs, and teams because I get satisfaction from seeing them continue to exist, evolve, and improve, and knowing that I had a hand in their success.

In the early 2000s, I owned a strategic brand implementation business. My team and I were brought into Fortune 500 tech companies that were moving from business-to-business sales to business-to-consumer sales. We would come into the company and up-level aspects of their marketing operations such as their corporate branding, product marketing, and channel management to drive the company into their new market. My success was defined by our ability to integrate our approach and the changes we had helped implement seamlessly into the corporate culture and systems of the company that had hired us...and then slip away. We would hand the new operational structure to a mature manager who could take it from there. I was by definition the change agent; long-term management required a different kind of leader.

Some leaders enjoy the thrill of the turnaround but feel deeply invested in managing for the long term. Before you make the decision to stay around, you need to ask yourself an important question: What is the best next step for my project, team, or organization?

Sometimes it is easy to become so focused on what is in front of you that you forget to lift your head and see the greater changes that are going on around you. As you were executing your turnaround, your company or the industry in which your organization operates was also in the process of changing. These days, significant changes seem to come more frequently, creating new markets, new competitors, and new opportunities. Other teams and organizations have been doing their own turnarounds and springing up to compete with you.

What is the future of your project, team, or organization in this new landscape? Do you have a specific vision for it? Could that future include linking with someone else's vision through a merger of teams or companies? You need to walk into the next phase not with dreams of empire building for yourself, but with a focus on long-term success for the entity you will be leading.

If you choose to stay, define specifically what you hope to accomplish in the next phase of growth or transformation. Depending on how long your turnaround took, enough time may have passed that you may have a new boss. You will have to advocate all over again for why you are the best person to lead this next phase of execution. Come up with a new vision for the future, determine new Jobs 1, 2, and 3, set new aggressive goals, and commit to reassessing your assets and decision trees to solidify your wins. I personally believe that if you choose to stay, it will be better to set a deadline for bringing this new vision to fruition versus entering an open-ended situation. Negotiate a reasonable timeline with your boss or board or whoever is in charge. Make commitments to deliver specific results or outcomes and to measure your progress and success with metrics.

Once you've delivered a successful turnaround, there's a financial benefit to staying on board. When things are going well, you tend to be rewarded with higher salaries and bonuses. That can be very attractive, especially after working so hard to bring stability to your project, team, or organization, which might have included running the operation and salaries with a lean budget. For some, financial stability might be driving their decision to stay. Others might not need that financial stability, but might prefer it. At the end of the day, you have to ask yourself what motivates you. For me, I value my legacy more than I do staying on the gravy train.

KNOWING WHEN IT IS TIME TO STEP ASIDE

If you decide to step aside once the turnaround is completed, then the next question you need to answer is "When?"

First, you need to assess where your head is at. Leading a turnaround is exhausting. This turnaround may have depleted your internal resources. During the transformation of FARE, travel was mentally exhausting for me. When you are the boss, it's hard to always be nice and to carry the burden of conducting non-stop negotiations and coming up with solutions. The additional lack of sleep and the physical wear and tear of weekly travel wore me out. When the global pandemic hit, and I had to stay home like everyone else, I got a second wind. I found myself meeting with more significant donors via Zoom as their schedules and mine were easier to accommodate.

Even if you got a chance to recharge during the turnaround process, it is important to acknowledge that the level of commitment required to pull off a turnaround takes its toll not only physically and mentally, but also in terms of your life. Positive people tend to remember the good and let the less positive moments fade into the background. When you are deciding the best time to leave, it's important to remember both.

Evaluate what you gave up personally to bring that future perfect scenario to existence. Did you miss spending time with family and friends? Or the chance to pursue outside interests that once fed your spirit? Whether the turnaround lasted six months or five years, you gave of yourself, and so did those around you, like your family. You have to ask yourself, "Do I still have the ability and flexibility to make the personal sacrifices required to continue?"

Even if you are willing to continue making personal sacrifices, do you still enjoy managing the day-to-day grind? As your project, team, or organization stabilizes, you must decide if you are comfortable no longer being the disrupter. Be honest with yourself. If the daily grind is starting to bother you instead of energizing you, it's time to step down. Do not dilute your legacy by overstaying your welcome. No one else gets to be Queen Elizabeth with a sixty-plus-year reign. Most leaders are more like the Iron Lady, Prime Minister Margaret Thatcher, who ushered in the aggressive economic change of the United Kingdom, but was pushed out by her own party after eleven years.

Overstaying your welcome may have other consequences. Once you've turned around your project, team, or organization, it likely opened the door to many opportunities for your team members. Keeping the best and brightest engaged in continuing the future you've taken such pains to make a reality is critical. But if you overstay your welcome, the path to leadership within your group becomes unclear. If you stay longer than you should, your heirs apparent might go somewhere else.

You've brought about great and positive change while leading the turnaround. Now it's time to focus on preserving your legacy. Do not become so obsessed with control that you lose sight of the fact that life gives all of us term limits. You do not get to be in charge forever—nor is it good for your project, team, or organization. Someday you have to let it go.

HANDING OVER THE MANTLE OF LEADERSHIP

At some point, the old guard must step down to allow new thought leaders to step forward. The very best leaders put in place transition plans well in advance to make this transition as smooth as possible. By grooming and mentoring talents in your group, you are not only teaching them how to see future opportunities for growth, but also ensuring that they remain committed to the dream you co-created. As Fortune 500 companies are quick to recognize, continuous renewal does not always include a change agent. In fact, if you built things right, your idea will continue to live on in the organization and be carried out by those you mentored and trained.

When I joined Intel in 1989, the tech giant was formalizing its succession planning process. I remember reading the main article in a *Newsweek* magazine that featured four faces on its cover. The headline asked who would be the heir apparent to Andy Grove, its then-legendary CEO. As in everything he did, Andy took a process-driven approach to identifying the right person to lead the organization in its new phase. Once Craig Barrett was selected, Andy slowly handed over the reins of the company by granting him authority *before* the transition. Wall Street and investors appreciated the kind of stability that move created.

Similarly, when Steve Jobs became ill, a succession plan for Apple became a high priority. He and the company focused on elevating Tim Cook and grooming him for the CEO job. In turn, Tim has focused on mentoring a new generation of leaders.

Thomas Donahue was CEO of the U.S. Chamber of Commerce for decades. He decided to stay on board into his eighties but groomed an efficient new president and CEO in Suzanne Clark. She was able to assume more and more tasks of leadership until she ascended to the top spot in 2021—and became the first woman to lead the U.S. Chamber of Commerce.

As these leaders prove, there's great value in a well-thought-out succession plan. But even if you are leading a project or team, not a tech giant or historical institution, grooming someone to take over when you are ready to go is critical. When you don't have a good plan in place, it creates turmoil and loses ground for the project or team you've put so much of yourself in.

Once you are ready to turn over the reins to the next person, do it cleanly. My father, who built a large institution from the ground up, believed that you had to be prepared to walk out the door at any time. You either handed over the mantle of leadership, or someone would force you to do so. He thought you should continue to give your all until that moment came so the changes you enacted would be preserved. But once you left, you should walk away on a high note.

When my father finally left his university post after many years, he *left*. He resisted the temptation to join the board or to keep a hand in some aspect of the operation. Instead, he gave his successors the ability and authority to fulfill their vision for the future. For my father, selfless leadership was at the heart of stronger institutions.

Making the decision to leave for good can be a hard line to take as many of your team members have invested so much in aligning their efforts with your vision and might feel very loyal. Many will reach out to ask you for advice on what to do with some aspect of the project or organization, particularly if leadership wants to make changes. Unless you are prepared to step back into the drama, leave it alone. It is not your job, nor is it fair to those who are now in charge, to get involved. Instead, be happy for the new leaders. Cheer them on. When I leave a project or organization and get calls like these, my answer is always "so-and-so is now in charge; it is their decision."

Handing over the mantle of leadership is easier when you have instituted internal processes that can sustain your project, team, or organization once you are gone. The method I described in this book not only helps you execute a turnaround, but also promotes a pattern for the future. It helps you embed a new vision, core competency, and decision trees in their DNA and set them up to weather changes positively for many years. No one lives forever. We and the projects, teams, and institutions we manage have a life span, too.

WINDING UP FOR THE NEXT PITCH

You've decided to leave. Now what?

If you can afford to do so, take some time off to regenerate. You just went through a grueling process with a lot of emotional swings. Get your head on straight before you move on to your next adventure.

If you don't have a mentor to help you brainstorm ideas for what you can do next, this might be the time to find someone. I was asked recently if there is a point in your career when you no longer need a mentor. I don't think so. You always need someone to talk through ideas or to learn from when tackling a new problem.

For example, I have been lucky enough to do a lot of things in my professional life, but until now, had never written a book. So I found new mentors to help me tackle this overwhelming task. I left my ego at the door and let them guide me as I moved through a process that was alien to me. A mentor can help you determine if it's time for you to tackle a new turnaround, try something new, or go back to positions like those you held before this chapter of your life.

Personally, I can't sit still. I love fixing things—I know that about myself. If you are as fortunate as I have been, you will arrive at a point in your life and career where you'll find yourself with the flexibility to engage from a place that touches your heart, where you feel you can make a difference. Between my time at PepsiCo and FARE, I recognized that I thrive when I can bring together political parties, corporate competitors, and disparate constituents to get things done that benefit society, create sustainable partnerships, and provide profitable business models. I am happiest representing public-private partnerships and nonprofits and moving them to higher levels of performance. I truly love to make a difference—and I found a great place to do that at FARE.

You may decide, however, that the success of this turnaround and your experience leading it opens new doors for you. Particularly if you led a whole organization through a turnaround, you might be approached about corporate director roles on the boards of publicly traded companies or nonprofits. Being a director requires new skills and a different mentality than being a C-suite executive. You will shift from having management responsibilities to providing fiduciary and governance oversight to companies and organizations. Unless you have previous experience in the space, a mentor on the board you are joining would be helpful as she or he can give you advice and support your entry as a leader at the table.

If you were forced to step in and lead your turnaround, you may come to the conclusion that once was enough for you. That is OK, too. Celebrate your wins and go back to doing the work you love to do. Not everyone wants to be in charge all the time. You may like being part of a team instead of leading it.

I believe God has a purpose for our life. He sees our entire timeline and sometimes gives us unique opportunities to make a difference or have an impact. Be proud of what you have achieved and keep driving towards results—even if you've chosen not to be in charge anymore. In the end, you'll enjoy the satisfaction of knowing you've lived life well and with meaning. This life experience, in fact, will make you the perfect mentor to the next generation of leaders tasked with solving intractable problems and righting things when they go south. I hope you share with them the biggest lesson of all: It is only through connecting with others' unique and diverse perspectives that we can arrive at the best possible solutions to the many challenges before us today and down the road.

ACKNOWLEDGMENTS

One of my life tenets is that you need to develop a best-of-class professional personal team to serve as resources in whatever project you involve yourself. A book does not get written or published by itself, nor does a turnaround happen through the actions of one person. As a result, I have a plethora of people to acknowledge.

First, I am indebted to my parents. I still hear my late father, Dr. Pierre Guillermin, who taught me how to visualize the future, manage with heart, and never give up. My mother, Louanne Guillermin, showed me how to build an expansive personal team and deploy my network to solve problems, help other people, and make the world a better place.

Second, I am thankful for my mentors. Craig Barrett taught me to apply manufacturing processes to solve problems not only in business, but also in philanthropy and government. In later years, Barbara Barrett would nominate me to be on boards on which she served and always encouraged me with advice and a reference. I was amazingly fortunate to meet this powerhouse couple so early in my life and appreciate the incredible foundation of credentials and experiences they facilitated for me and that helped me build a fascinating career.

Secretary Elaine Chao and I met through the Reagan White House. Elaine has always been available to me whenever I called with a question or a request for help. Admiral Marsha "Marty" Evans became my wise counsel in situations that required a deft hand and great care. I came to know Ambassador Nancy Brinker and Judy Black better mid-career; they have accomplished amazing things in life and have helped me to determine the best way to approach political complexities.

Dani Mackey, my personal PR consultant, encouraged me to write a book and diligently made sure I took every step that was required to do it. I am forever grateful for her introduction to Rohit Bhargava, publisher of Ideapress Publishing, who taught me how to write, publish, and promote a book, providing detailed input throughout the process. Rohit's best advice was to hire Genoveva Llosa as my editor. She became my tutor and guide. Genoveva and I shared a common philosophy about life and business that enabled us to achieve the ultimate mind meld, as she knew what I wanted to say and helped me say it better.

I rely heavily on my husband, Jim, and my sister, Michelle, for assessing ideas and concepts and figuring out the quantitative side of each equation. Over the years, I have learned never to doubt my sister's ability to identify the initial place where an organization started to unravel nor my husband's ability to tolerate and support me when I am at the toughest stage of a turnaround.

I send a big smooch and hug to my daughter, Helen-Anne, who had a mother who was frequently on the road and sometimes distracted, but who loves her dearly.

Finally, I thank those who were in the trenches with me in each turnaround referenced in this book. They are best at what they do, and many have been willing to participate in repeat performances, always ready to help me dissect the next big problem and establish the infrastructure to move an organization to a higher level of performance.

For me, the core of who I am and who I've become started at the Reagan White House and at Intel Corporation. Hats off to my fellow Reaganites: Susan Bari, Charmaine Crouse, Kathleen Durkee, Julia Ciorletti Grant, Charlie Ingersoll, Anita McBride, Mark Robbins, Dennis Stephens, the late Tag Tognalli, Bob Tuttle, Eric Vautour, and Michele Woodward. I learned a lot from my Intel friends, with whom I shared objectives and key results: Nancy Ballinger, Stefani Bloch, Richard "Dick" Boucher, Naomi Chavez, Patricia Houden, Mike Maibach, the late Paul Otellini, Jessica Rocha, and Jackie Whittier.

U.S. participation at the 2005 Aichi World Expo was truly a team sport. I appreciate the dedication of my colleagues, including the U.S. Pavilion staff and guides, U.S. Department of State, U.S. Foreign and Commercial Service, Toyota Corporation, Bush '43 alumni, and fellow ambassadors from participating countries. A few specific people without whom I would not have been successful include the late Ambassador Howard Baker, Daniel Berkowitz, Jo Cooper, Tom Donahue, Mark Felton, Jerry Giaquinta, DiAnne Owen Graham, Amy Malerba Hemingway, the Hon. Patricia De Stacy Harrison, Travis Horel, Julia Hochbaum, Ambassador and Mrs. Ryozo Kato, Connie Lockwood, Mel Lukens, Ambassador Mike Michalak, Gary Oba, Jim Ogul, Secretary Colin Powell, Dina Powell, Ambassador Thomas Schieffer, Ben Shuster, Tom Snitch, Toshiaki "Tag" Taguchi, Dr. Shoichiro Toyoda, David John Tuck, David Vennett, and Doug West.

The Healthy Weight Commitment Foundation (HWCF) required massive teamwork and cooperation. Thank you to the sixteen companies who joined the HWCF market-place pledge: Bumble Bee Foods, LLC; Campbell Soup Company; ConAgra Foods; General Mills, Inc.; Kellogg Company; Kraft Foods, Inc. (now Kraft Foods and Mondelēz International); Mars, Incorporated; McCormick & Company, Inc.; Nestlé USA; PepsiCo, Inc.; Post Foods/ Ralston Foods, LLC; Hillshire Brands (previously Sara Lee Corporation); The Coca-Cola Company; The Hershey Company; The J.M. Smucker Company; and Unilever.

A huge virtual hug to my core team and daily advisors at HWCF: Mary Ellen Brown, Hank Cardello, Emily Cullum, Alli Delano, Eileen Doherty, Rebecca Feldman, Michelle Guillermin, Becky Johnson, Clark Judge, Nabeelah Khan, Bill Macleod, Sean McBride, Catherine Trinh Michael, Val Newcomb, Susan Ralston, Mary Rollins, and Chris Zagar. Kudos to our vendors: Discovery Education, White House Writers Group, Edelman Digital, Signal Marketing Group, and Saatchi and Saatchi. We are grateful to the Robert Wood Johnson Foundation for serving as the independent outside scientific evaluator, with special thanks to Elaine Arkin, Dr. Jim Marks, Dr. Tracy Orleans, and Dr. Risa Lavizzo-Mourey. First Lady Michelle Obama's team created the momentum: Debra "Deb" Eschmeyer, Sam Kass, Robin Schepper, and Larry

Soler. The HWCF Working Team kept sixteen competitors moving forward in lock step. A special thanks to those with whom I spoke often: Adam Adams, Rhona Applebaum, Elizabeth Avery, Mark Baynes, Bob Earl, Hamed Faridi, Ron Graf, Ryan Guthrie, Chavanne Hanson, Dave Melbourne, Kim Nelson, Mary Sophos, Julia Sabin, Julia Sessoms, and Derek Yach. A special thank you to our visionary leader Indra Nooyi, my daily mentor Sandy Douglas, and the board members who were always there for me—Bert Alfonso, JP Bilbrey, C.J. Fraleigh, Paul Grimwood, Ric Jurgens, David Mackay, Denise Morrison, Ken Powell, Tim Smucker, and Dave West. An appreciation for our association leaders: Pam Bailey, Susan Neely, and Leslie Sarasin. Finally, a shout out to Drs. Chor San H Khoo and Claire Wang, who had the epiphany that it was all about calories as we met in the McCormick Idea Lab one wintry day.

At FARE, we are building our success around our core competencies in food allergy research, education, and advocacy. A special thanks to Denise and Dave Bunning, who believed in the plan and backed it 200 percent. Sending the warmest of hugs to the core turnaround team: Vanita Boswell, Dr. Tom Casale, Tina Dodge, Sherry Fazio, Nurry Hong, Karen Roche,

ACKNOWLEDGMENTS

Dominique Rodriguez-Sawyer, and Michael Trager. My sincere appreciation to those who helped me learn important food allergy facts: Emily Brown, Nancy Gregory, Jen Jobrack, Lianne Mandelbaum, Mary Jane Marchisotto, Thomas Silvera, and Gwen Smith. I want to highlight my gratitude for those who served on the FARE growth team: Jonathan Cane, Steve Danon, Michael Frazier, Dr. Ruchi Gupta, Jim Lutzweiler, Susan Ralston, Dr. Bruce Roberts, and Bart Snell. Thank you to FARE Medical Advisors: Dr. Kari Nadeau, Dr. Wayne Shreffler, and Dr. Brian Vickery. I also extend my gratitude to current members of the FARE Board of Directors, including Dr. Milton Brown, Leigh Feuerstein, Alan Hartman, Helen Jaffe, Rebecca Lainovic, Adam Miller, Rob Rich, and Mary Weiser, and to former members of the Board of Directors who were instrumental getting me onboarded, including Janet Atwater, John Hannan, and Rob Nichols. I thank the Board of Governor co-chairs Kim Hartman and David Crown, PhD; Board of National Ambassador co-chairs Karin Teglia and Kim Yates; and transformational donors who made early commitments, Ben and Hillary Carter, Talia and Andrew Day, Alan and Kim Hartman, Helen and David Jaffe, Peter Kolchinsky, PhD, the Kellen family, Don and Kathy Levin, Adam

Miller, Dr. Chris Olsen and Robert Small, the Naddisy Foundation, Diana and Ira Riklis, Cari and Michael Sacks, the Sunshine Charitable Foundation, and Mary and Marc Weiser. Most important, I want to recognize FARE staff, the FARE Clinical Network, our partners, support group leaders, and advocates whose tenacity and diligence keep the food allergy community safe.

Finally, where would I be without my personal and professional team on whom I rely regularly for advice and support? Thank you to Sylvia Acevedo, Judith Ayres, Bobby Burchfield, Ana Carcani Rold, Cordell Carter, Mary Kate Cary, Donna Casey, Stephanie Childs, Marlene Colucci, Kendra Davenport, Annie Dickerson, Auren Hoffman, Terry Huang, Paige Healey, Loretta Lepore, Betsy Lewis, Wonya Lucas, Megan Medica, Caren Merrick, Sandra Miley, Terry Neese, Lisa Nelson, Sally Pipes, Kimberly Reed, Rob Reid, Heidi Roizen, Martha Ryan, Liz Sara, Betsy Smith, Lisa Spies, Robin Sprague, Elizabeth Thompson, Jill and Alex Vogel, Deborah Wince Smith, Julianna Shaw, and Bridgett Wagner—and family John, Gingy, Bob, Beth, and Bo Gable.

I wouldn't be here today—in a meaningful career I enjoy—if I had not met these amazing leaders and built the friendships that give me strength. Thank you all!

ENDNOTES

1   https://www.rwjf.org/en/library/articles-and-news/2009/07/f-as-in
    -fat-2009.html

2   https://usefyi.com/salesforce-history/

3   https://www.who.int/news-room/fact-sheets/detail/tobacco

4   https:// www.casaa.org/education/vaping/historical-timeline-of-
    electronic-cigarettes/

5   https:// www.casaa.org/education/vaping/historical-timeline-of-
    electronic-cigarettes/

6   https://businessinsider.com/juul-congress-e-cigs-target-teens

7   https://www.tobaccofreekids.org/assets/factsheets/0398.pdf

8   https://www.wsj.com/articles/during-covid-19-lockdowns-people-went
    -back-to-smoking-11611829803

9   https://www.rwjf.org/en/library/articles-and-news/2014/01/major-food
    --beverage-companies-remove-6-4-trillion-calories--fro.html

10 https://s3.amazonaws.com/media.hudson.org/files/publications
    /HWCFcompanyGrowth_09132014fPPTFINAL.pdf

11 https://www.bie-paris.org/site/en/what-is-an-expo

12 https://www.fooddive.com/news/bolthouse-farms-chief-rebuilding
    -company-after-wrong-marriage-to-campbell/566578/

13 https://www.latimes.com/archives/la-xpm-2000-apr-14-mn-19453-story
    .html

14 https://www.forbes.com/sites/moorinsights/2018/10/12/all-rise-john
    -medica/?sh=6741cf234f41

15 Andy Grove, *Only the Paranoid Survive: How to Exploit the Crisis Points
    That Challenge Every Company* (New York: Doubleday Business, 1996).

16 Andy Grove, *Only the Paranoid Survive: How to Identify and Exploit the Crisis Points that Challenge Every Business* (New York: Currency/ Doubleday, 1996).

17 Jim Collins and Jerry I. Porras, *Build to Last: Successful Habits of Visionary Companies* (New York: HarperBusiness, 1994).

18 John Doerr, *Measure What Matters: How Google, Bono, and the Gates Foundation Rock the World with OKRs* (New York: Portfolio, 2018).

19 https://www.nestle.com/csv/what-is-csv

20 https://2012-2017.usaid.gov/news-information/frontlines/50-years-and-food-security/pepsi-and-chickpeas-interview-derek-yach

21 https://www.coca-colacompany.com/news/coca-colas-polar-bears

INDEX

INDEX

INDEX

INDEX

INDEX

ABOUT THE AUTHOR

LISA GABLE is recognized worldwide as a turnaround mastermind. As CEO of several organizations and as a former U.S. ambassador, United Nations delegate, and advisor to Fortune 500 companies, Lisa has orchestrated and executed the successful turnarounds of well-known private and public organizations in many industries and sectors. She is highly regarded in business, political, and philanthropic circles for her ability to tackle difficult issues directly with discipline and diplomacy.

Over the years, Lisa's proven turnaround methods have helped her move organizations to higher levels of performance by creating sustainable partnerships and profitable business models that have brought together political parties, corporate competitors, and even disparate nations. She is currently the CEO of FARE, the world's premier organization fighting food allergies. Prior to leading FARE, she was a senior advisor at PepsiCo and president of the Healthy Weight Commitment

Foundation, where she worked on cross-sector solutions to improve intractable public health issues. From 1994 to 2009, she was a founding principal of The Brand Group, an advisory firm dedicated to helping companies such as Apple, Gap Inc., Intel, Oracle, Radisson Hotels, GI Film Festivals, and more implement change strategies.

In 2004, she was appointed by President George W. Bush as the first woman in the World Fair's 150-year history to direct the U.S. Pavilion, a 100 percent non-federally funded, $33.7 million operation with more than seventy employees. She completed operations with the first budget surplus in the history of the World's Fair, an achievement publicly recognized in a U.S. Senate proclamation in 2005. Earlier in her career, Lisa worked in high tech as corporate identity manager at Intel, in the White House as deputy associate director of presidential personnel, and in the U.S. Department of Defense as a special assistant in technology transfer policy.

Lisa was named one of the Ten Most Innovative Businesswomen in 2020 by *Business Berg* magazine. An entrepreneur and mentor, Lisa acts deliberately to move organizations and individuals toward their full potential. In the past, she served as the founding chair of the board of directors for the Foundation for a Smoke-Free World; was a national trustee of the Boys and Girls Club of America and a member of the board of directors of Girls Scouts of the USA; a trustee of Thunderbird School of Global Management; and a member of the National Academy of Medicine IOM Roundtable on Obesity Solutions. She is also a mentor in organizations such as the Rare as One Project, a Chan Zuckerberg Initiative.

A published writer, Lisa is regularly featured in the media and for four years was a regularly scheduled guest with Lifetime TV's national morning program, *The Balancing Act*.

A proud mom to a Montessori teacher, Lisa lives in Washington, D.C., with her husband, a high-tech entrepreneur.

A CONVERSATION WITH LISA GABLE

(Adapted from an interview on The Non-Obvious Book Review, hosted by Rohit Bhargava)

Lisa, I always like to start with this question: What makes your book "nonobvious"?

What makes the book not obvious is its approach to turnarounds: It combines the discipline I learned early on in my career working in manufacturing operations at Intel Corporation with the art of diplomacy and persuasion I mastered working at the White House, the Defense Department, and the State Department as a U.S. Ambassador.

You have such a fascinating background. In the book, one of the interesting perspectives you share is about the importance of thinking like a process engineer. What do you mean by that, and what's unique about how a process engineer thinks?

A process engineer always thinks within the context of workflows and timelines—they work on producing a set of deliverables that build on each other. They also use statistical process control to see whether the process is working, if it is as efficient as possible, and how to solve problems with it. As I "peel back the onion" of a lot of organizations that have headed south or a project that's not moving forward, it's easier for me to see where they weren't using the right processes or where they weren't really thinking about the variables when I have my process engineer hat on. The variables are a critical piece people often fail to account for. Where are all the different opportunities for something to go awry? Sometimes organizations add so many factors into their success strategy that it gets unwieldy. In most cases, they are better off streamlining and leveraging their stronger assets as opposed to operating towards perfection, which then requires identifying and using a lot of different mechanisms to reach your end goal. The more complexity you add, the greater opportunity for something to go off course.

In Turnaround, you start by identifying why things go south in the first place. One of the reasons you shared that I found surprising was the belief that money can solve all problems. Why do so many leaders believe that, and why is it wrong?

Yes, too much money is sometimes one of the biggest issues. It's not only that wealthy individuals and some CEOs throw money at the problem, but also that they think the problem is "easy" and can be solved by installing a person who has been successful in other roles and giving them lots of money to fix the problem. What they don't understand is that you are better off requiring people to work their way out of a box because you are confronting an effort that's completely unraveled. You have to break the organization or project down and put it back together again. The new version of it you create must be designed to live and breathe after you step away from it. If you're throwing money at it, you are not focused on fixing the problem. Instead, you create bigger problems through further investment as you continue to bet on new directions. When people put too much money into a failing situation, they are not forced to rank and rate the assets they have and the activities and initiatives they engage in—instead they just extend them. Working your way out of the box forces you to prioritize. It forces you to make hard decisions. If you make those hard decisions immediately, you are more protected during an economic downturn. You're in a much better place for your organization to continue to grow and prosper in a sustainable fashion.

Another common corporate challenge you expose is how often leaders make self-interested or "empire-building" decisions. What are some examples of those types of decisions, and how can leaders avoid those?

When things are headed south, you should spend the time to understand why you keep running into problems. If you put your own self-interest above the interest of the organization, it's not going to work. In some cases, the problem might be that you are overspending on things that directly benefit you. Perhaps you like throwing big events, like galas or conferences, so you can be the center of attention. That was a significant issue I discovered when managing the United States' involvement in the 2005 World Expo (formerly known as the World's Fair). Those who had led the Expo in previous years had gotten caught up in the pomp and circumstances—the elegant dinners, the extravagant shows—and forgotten the purpose of the Expo: to strengthen economic development and long-term diplomatic ties with other nations.

When you prioritize your self-interest, you also risk making decisions based on your own ambitions, not on the good of the organization you are leading. We see this often in how CEOs spend public relations dollars. They may not be as focused on building the public conversation to support the long game, but instead are looking for quick headlines.

When you're focused on you, you're not focused on the organization. You're not really spending the time to understand why people in the organization may not be happy or why your customers aren't happy.

Instead, you're thinking of the short term. How do I grow something that fits my specific (personal) need?

Sometimes leaders will design an organizational effort because it benefits their exit plan—it builds their personal reputation and résumé in anticipation of the next job. Well, if you're doing a turnaround, you want to design your efforts so that the process or program lives and breathes, grows and thrives, beyond your time within the organization.

In the book, I tell the story of an organization that I helped build—a school. For the past thirty years, I've checked on the health of the school and its performance every single year. I'm so proud of the fact that I left it in a place where it could grow beyond me. And that's the important thing to remember. It's not about you. You are the steward of other people's money—your shareholders', investors', and donors' money. Your actions must support activities that benefit the organization, the people, and the community you serve.

Oftentimes leaders are just focused on the last quarter's results or on the quick wins—they are stuck on short-term thinking. Why do they do that instead of playing what you describe in the book as the "long game"?

I've seen many situations where leaders were focused on their big win—making sure that they made a mark that's associated with their name and their tenure. The person executes their big win. They get a lot of accolades. In many cases, they get a new job because they've actually used the big win not for the purpose of the organization, but to get the next big role. Yet when they depart the organization, that "win" can't survive them. And that deliverable on which they spent so much time and seemed so committed to dies as soon as they depart.

It has no legs. It has no depth. They have not thought that you need to strategically implement the major win in a manner that builds the strength of the organization, not only within their unit, but also across the entire organization. If you go for the quick win, what you have to remember is that the win should be only a set-up towards something that needs to continue after you've left the organization.

The first chapter of your book opens with the story of Indra Nooyi, the former CEO of PepsiCo. Take us behind the scenes and tell us how that moment was an example of what you spotlight in the book as the first step of the turnaround method—"visualizing the future"?

In 2008, Indra stepped forward at a major industry event attended by many CEOs. She challenged them to join her in making significant changes in their product port-folios and philanthropic spending to help decrease the rise of obesity. What Indra knew is that these companies had made a lot of changes in their product portfolios already, but there was no way to measure the effective-ness of these changes. Indra saw a future where the industry wasn't getting attacked by the public health community for contributing to the problem of obesity, but instead where public health and business were work-ing arm in arm—not fighting.

She recognized that a certain segment of the indus-try significant enough to have an impact on changing the food supply needed to be involved. And so, she chal-lenged the entire leadership in the food and beverage industry. Sixteen food and beverage company CEOs joined her in an effort that would become the Healthy Weight Commitment Foundation, which I would run for them. The sixteen companies represented 35 percent of the foods and beverages sold in America.

The CEOs analyzed what their companies were doing and how much money they were spending in the commu-nities. They realized that if they combined and aligned their spending towards very specific outcomes, the U.S. would see significant change in the places where they manufactured and sold products. The volume of change would be magnified and multiplied by sixteen food and beverage companies making investments around similar goals. At the time, the food and beverage industry was facing an effort to tax some beverages—a "sugar tax"—and potentially to restrict sodium in their products. It was critical that they band together to make enough changes in their products to secure the credibility to have conversations with legislators and leaders in government.

A big part of the book is about collaboration and getting buy-in. I loved that you were not overly optimistic on this. You openly acknowledge that sometimes you just won't be able to take certain people with you. They just won't go along for the ride. They won't agree with your course of direction. What do you do in that situation?

There are three types of people who don't get on board. First, there are the people who just are going to resist you, oppose you. It may be jealousy about the public position of your organization or about your leadership position. Or they're so competitive they don't see how they can be more successful working with you. Second, you have individuals who let their egos get in the way. They lead so much with their ego that they can't possibly function well in a coalition. And that's problematic because you have to sacrifice your own ego to be successful as a group. You have to make compromises that you're uncomfortable with to get people to move on board.

And finally, there are people that you try to get on board, but the manner in which you operate is very different. You try so hard to merge your ideals with theirs and align your spending with their spending. You personally like them a great deal. Sometimes it just doesn't work. In those cases, it is important to depart the relationship in a diplomatic way. Acknowledge the fact that the relationship is not working. Encourage everyone not to take things personally. It's just business. You respect those people. You're grateful and thank them for their participation in the conversation. And maybe five years later you find an opportunity to work with them. So leave the relationship with your head held high, respecting the other individual, respecting where they're at, and just acknowledge the fact that things don't work out sometimes.

This is also a good point to remember when employees leave your organization. When I have a senior staff member leave, I buy them a personal present from me—something that will be really special for that individual, something that they will personally value. I congratulate them on their new job. With a sendoff that acknowledges the good they did in their work with you, individuals are happier with the relationship. I then stay in touch with them. Why not? You need good people throughout your life, and I'm old enough now to know how many times I've run into people over and over again.

It's clear throughout the book that you personally don't attach a lot of your own ego to why something is successful or not. That point really came to life when you talked about running the U.S. presence at the 2005 World Expo in Japan. Apparently the U.S. had not participated in nor hosted a World Expo on budget for more than one hundred years. Yet you did it. What was your secret?

The most important thing for me is getting the job done the right way: fiscally responsibly, with appropriate governance, and delivering a big result. When the White House offered me the position as U.S. Commissioner General, I was aware the United States was entering our 2005 Aichi World Expo engagement as the very last country to sign up to participate. In retrospect, I have to laugh, as my team and I were reminded of that every time our flag was the last to enter a room after 199 other country flags. At diplomatic events, our team was constantly reminded that we had been the last ones to sign up.

As a result, I had to move quickly. I was focused on one fact: We had to build the U.S. Pavilion in six months and have it ready for millions of people to visit. Plus, I had to have the funds in place to pay for the costs of U.S. engagement. Whenever I am facing a tight time frame in which I must be successful in a very public way, I get "in the zone." I am extremely focused on the top three things I need to get done. And as a result, I don't really think about myself personally within that mix. I'm just driving towards the results and making sure I am working my way through problems and building relationships so I can deliver on my promise.

The first problem was how we were going to pay for anything that involved my participation as U.S. Commissioner General. A 1998 law stipulated that public monies could not cover a number of expenses. My husband and I ended up picking up a significant portion of the tab. So there was a personal reason I wasn't hosting lavish lunches and dinners: I would have had to pay for it!

Also there was the fact that I'm scrawny! I don't eat a lot. I forget to eat when I am focused on getting stuff done.

I recall a moment I came back stateside to have meetings, and my State Department colleagues were talking about the previous Commissioner Generals who had represented the U.S. They were concerned about their spending, particularly their meal budgets. They were concerned that I might repeat the same mistakes.

The one thing about all these men—by the way, every commissioner general before me was a man—is that they loved the big dinners and entertaining. They valued dinners. I didn't and made it clear that my sole focus would be on economic development, delivering rich cultural programming, and most important, ensuring we paid 100 percent of our bills on time.

I bet none of them got sworn in at Kinko's! I loved that story in the book. What was that moment like?

You are right. I needed to be sworn into the office of Commissioner General immediately in order to meet a tight signing deadline with the Japanese government. I asked folks what I needed to do to be "official." The answer was that I needed a notary to swear me into office before I flew to Japan. So I was calling around and asking who had a notary. I finally called Kinko's. The person who answered said, "We have a notary." I drove to a Kinko's in Northern Virginia with my little piece of paper. The lady at the desk asked, "What am I swearing you in for?" And so, I told her. She gathered everyone in the store for an impromptu ceremony. People were on the copy machines, and in the process of buying stationary and office supplies. She went in the back office, found this tiny little plastic stand that had three American flags, and set it out on the checkout counter. I took the oath of office, and everybody in the Kinko's clapped. I then ran back to the State Department and gave them the signed paperwork that indicated I could leave immediately for Japan as an official representative of the United States with the rank of U.S. Ambassador. I just like to get stuff done. The big hurrah wasn't as important to me as efficiency.

We were able to cut out a great deal of expense as that philosophy became core to how I ran my team. Unfortunately, I've heard about some of the cost overruns at the last few World Fairs. They weren't as focused on what they needed to do to pay for the Expo. For me it is personal. If I tell you I will do something on budget, I am determined to keep that promise—even if it requires personal sacrifice.

You advise readers to audit and rank all of the assets that they've got. And you have this really interesting physical way of doing that. As a leader of a turnaround, how do you decide what is worth keeping and what is worth losing?

The idea originally came from my time rebranding large companies for fifteen-plus years in Silicon Valley. When I arrived in Santa Clara in the early 1990s, I ran Intel's corporate identity program and completely re-engineered it to effectively realize cost savings, as well as ensure that we could legally own and support our brands in a manner that wouldn't risk losing ownership of our trademarks—a problem Intel had already experienced.

With big identity projects, it's a very physical process. You're reviewing stationery, signage, magazine ads, digital ads, digital interfaces, and more. I trained myself to look at the characteristics that bound those visuals together and identified ways that they could be grouped according to their purpose—target audience, information conveyed, functional purpose, and so on. We would literally build out these big boards, take the different visual imagery that represented the company, and show our clients the discombobulated way in which they presented themselves to the world. Many of them hadn't really noticed it. When we brought the board out, there would be an "OMG" moment.

I was trained in this very visual process of analysis. I took the process as I moved from corporate identity management into brand management on the web. (Yes, I'm old enough that I actually remember the launch of the first commercial websites, websites built for consumer purposes.) The problem I immediately saw was that we would need to take every functional area of the company and create a path to build an interface for our core business in the new World Wide Web.

This was not an easy process. A commercial bank is a perfect example. Back then, banks managed their consumer business mostly through physical retail operations and a high degree of customer engagement. As we were designing these first online interfaces, we realized we were trying to force consumers to have an experience based on the traditional manner in which the company managed behind the scenes. Using our visualization process, we would analyze the user experience to ensure the way the bank was managing things in no way, shape, or form made its way into the consumer's point of view. That seems so logical today, but it was an epiphany in the 1990s.

Since I advanced in my career through these two categories of business—the origins of corporate identity and the first round of web design—I always default to that "physical" process. For example, once my team working with a big Fortune 100 company discovered it had 150 different legal relationships with their channels. Basically, each sales team would alter and cut a slightly different contract to make their channel partner sign the deal. We took those contracts and started grouping them, circling and highlighting the variances. Then we grouped them by characteristics, literally stacking them on the conference table. That physical process allowed us to streamline the clients' legal process very quickly. We transitioned the client from 150 different licenses to three basic channel marketing agreements with tiered benefits.

For me, the physicality of being able to see something is important—even if you don't use the floor or conference table "stacking method" to audit your assets and processes. Perhaps you are working with a team that is in different geographies and use a spreadsheet or a Word document to do your "virtual stacking." Sometimes it still helps to print the thing out, lay documents on the floor, and then start seeing what pieces aren't fitting together.

I love this. My method is so similar! I tend to use a lot of Post-it notes, tear things out of magazines, and move stuff around physically to curate trends for my work. And you're right, our brains are trained to work in that way. You write in Turnaround that "every business or philanthropy is in a competition." What do you mean by that?

We're all competing for resources. We're competing for people. We're competing for money. We are competing for a voice in the conversation. Everything in life is a competition. Now what's interesting about that is personally I only care about competitions that matter. I am a horrible person to have over for game night because I really don't care if I lose Monopoly or a game of cards. It doesn't matter to me if I win.

OK, I'm not picking you as my partner....

Winning a game doesn't matter to me whatsoever. But I do care greatly about making sure that the people who work for me have a seat at the table. I want my team to be the ones getting the awards or being recognized as thought leaders. My goal is to change the terms of the debate in such a way that we actually own the conversation and drive it in a new, innovative direction.

Work in philanthropy, government, or business is always a competition because you are benchmarking your performance at all times against your peer group, best-of-class organizations, and even a wide array of organizations. You're constantly asking, Why? Why were they able to get to where they got to, and what am I doing wrong? It's not necessarily that I'm hyper-competitive—I believe in the importance of collaboration. For me, it's the success factor. I don't like to not have something *not* work. I twitch if it doesn't work. And so, I am always benchmarking.

Let's shift to the third step of your turnaround method: creating a path from the present to the future. You offer a great tool that you call the decision tree to do this. What is a decision tree and how do you use it?

A decision tree helps you group things and determine how many different outcomes can be delivered by narrowing the critical pathways. The process forces you to make hard decisions and focus. If you initially begin to develop a decision tree, and it leads you to ten different decision points, that means there's something wrong with your processes. It means that you're not focused on the primary objectives of the organizations or the end game that's going to change the dynamic and enable you to move that organization forward to a new level of competition.

A decision tree is another visualization process that allows people to see the route to the decisions they must make. I find decision trees help clarify things in people's minds. (Isn't that why we like whiteboarding?) It forces everybody into a yes/no or go/no go answer. It also enables you to ground your team in using the same decision-making process. Everyone must answer certain questions to qualify for more resources, a new logo, marketing support for a new program, and the like. Building decision trees is another process I learned back in the late 1980s, early 1990s at Intel.

And now we're at the fourth step of the turnaround method: Execute with speed, confidence, and heart. Talk about what that means and how readers can do it.

If you followed my four-step process, you have visualized your future, you've audited what you have, and you've created a decision tree, so everybody in your organization or project understands how you make decisions at the organization: These are the things we're going to do.

These are the things we're *not* going to do at this point. You've got a streamlined process. You can stop revisiting your decisions at every turn, which allows you to move quickly in executing your turnaround.

In many cases, I have had very short windows to turn an organization or a project around. I have taken over organizations and discovered that they are in the red operationally. I've had to quickly restructure them, and sometimes I've even had to change the composition of their boards. In those moments when you realize you're in dire straits, it becomes very important to move with speed. The agility often comes from collaboration. You recognize you don't have to own everything. Shared goals benefit everyone. And you're confident in your decisions because you're not questioning them constantly. You're not saying, "Well, what if we did it this way instead?" Well, because you just looked through your decision tree, and it shows you couldn't go in certain directions. Those options are officially off the table. The tools I offer in the book give readers confidence not only in making decisions, but also executing them with heart. It is important to remember that someone is going to be impacted by what you do. It doesn't matter if you are in the U.S. government, serving a quasi-governmental organization, working at a company, or running a philanthropic effort. If you are changing the organization's operation dramatically, your decisions will affect a human being. While you are optimizing processes, you need to be tough. But you also must recognize good people can get caught in the turmoil and be kind.

Big companies have the financial resources to help redeployed individuals with job training programs, résumé writing workshops, or outplacement programs. But the reality is most organizations don't have that flexibility or the financial resources to invest in a significant level of support. People are "on their own."

If people are departing because their role no longer fits in the organization or project, then treat them decently and with respect upon their exit. Be supportive and offer a good recommendation. It may not be their fault that the organization or project you walked into isn't functioning in an optimal way. When I execute a turnaround, I offer to have one-on-ones with people impacted and leaving the organization. I offer to mentor them. I ask other people to mentor them.

You close the book by talking about ending on a high note, wrapping up the work you're doing, and understanding when it's time to walk away. How can leaders make sure that the turnaround they institute doesn't immediately fall apart after they leave?

When I take on a turnaround, I'm very transparent about my planned length of stay. Sometimes I indicate to a board or a client that I'm with them for a set period of time. I discuss my commitment to get the organization to a specific level of performance by the end of my engagement. We have an honest conversation about developing a succession plan. I paint a picture of what the next phase might look like for the organization. I articulate what the organization will ultimately need to do to replace me. Those who have worked with me know that I am direct when I articulate the future I see for the organizations.

Management may choose to accept my recommendation, or they may choose not to. That is up to them or the board. The key is that when I walk out the door, the board and leadership feel ownership of the next evolution of the operation.

I began using this straightforward process of

articulating my engagement against a timeline when I ran a brand management consulting practice in Silicon Valley. During the 1990s, we were helping tech companies move from a B2B (or business-to-business) to a B2C (or business-to-consumer) model. Executives would bring my team into the organization to up-level or reposition the strategic intent of an existing part of the company, whether it was marketing, channel marketing, or brand management. Doing this works takes a different type of leadership than leading a department or unit long-term. You need somebody who's entrepreneurial, who's thinking outside the box, and who has experience in markets that are different than internal resources. So we would bring a team that had no "skin in the game." They were outsiders who were not protecting their turf. Our goal was solely focused on moving the organization to a new way of doing business. That requires making some hard changes and forcing an organization to let favorite practices go. Sometimes that is hard for companies to do those changes with internal resources—an insider might face resistance while an outsider might be given a bit more leeway due to their expertise and the fact that they ultimately will leave, so they are not viewed as internal competition.

My team and I were clear that, once we moved the

organization or business unit to the next level, we would hand over this new operational model to someone who was a good general manager. We would set a timeline for when we would walk away, having removed the barriers to success and having trained and realigned the internal teams.

The key to ending on a high note is to be professional, transparent, and honest with your boss or management team when you believe it is the right time for you to leave. On the flip side, your boss and board need to respect that transparency and value an appropriate transition. Mutual respect is required. The other key is to develop your exit in a process-oriented way that equals the professional manner in which you entered the organization. You want the new prototype that you've created or the new future that you visualized to survive upon your departure. Or else, why in the world did you go through all this effort?

Recorded in May 2021 as a live episode of **The Non-Obvious Book Review,** *hosted by author and trend curator Rohit Bhargava.*